"Decisions made by young men and women may have profound consequences for their education, their health, their career, indeed their eternity. Dr. Daniel Egeler poignantly notes that young people have tremendous potential and desire to positively influence our world. Although mentoring requires sacrifice and commitment, mentors can play a significant role in maximizing the impact of millennials. Dr. Egeler's brief treatise is not only refreshing, but it also encourages adults to serve as mentors. Just as Paul mentored Timothy, developing his confidence and competence, mentors can and should do the same for millennials. This is a valuable and provocative text addressing the role of mentoring in positively shaping our future."

—J. DIRK NELSON, PH.D., assistant vice president
for academic affairs, LeTourneau University

"This is an absolute-read for any parent or worker involved with the next generation. It is obvious that Dan Egeler has been at both ends of the mentoring spectrum. His illustrations and suggestions will help anyone who truly cares about the millennial generation and what we each leave behind."

—DR. RON CLINE, chairman, HCJB World Radio

"Christian leaders appreciate the rewards of successful mentoring relationships with emerging generations—they just don't always do it effectively. Here are some answers to that dilemma! *Mentoring Millennials* provides a wealth of practical helps and insights for developing relationships in a postmodern age. Dr. Egeler's book is thought-provoking, well-written, and engaging. The combination of personal experiences and scriptural teaching presents a solid approach for mentoring a generation that is much misunderstood, but has great potential."

—DR. PETER N. NANFELT, president,
The Christian and Missionary Alliance

"Dan Egeler aptly portrays the critical importance of mentoring and the unique approach necessary for the younger generation. A great book for understanding and mentoring millennials."

—DR. JOE HALE, president and founder,
Network of International Christian Schools, Inc.

MENTORING MILLENNIALS

SHAPING THE NEXT HERO GENERATION

Dr. Daniel Egeler

NAVPRESS®

BRINGING TRUTH TO LIFE

OUR GUARANTEE TO YOU

We believe so strongly in the message of our books that we are making this quality guarantee to you. If for any reason you are disappointed with the content of this book, return the title page to us with your name and address and we will refund to you the list price of the book. To help us serve you better, please briefly describe why you were disappointed. Mail your refund request to: NavPress, P.O. Box 35002, Colorado Springs, CO 80935.

The Navigators is an international Christian organization. Our mission is to reach, disciple, and equip people to know Christ and to make Him known through successive generations. We envision multitudes of diverse people in the United States and every other nation who have a passionate love for Christ, live a lifestyle of sharing Christ's love, and multiply spiritual laborers among those without Christ.

NavPress is the publishing ministry of The Navigators. NavPress publications help believers learn biblical truth and apply what they learn to their lives and ministries. Our mission is to stimulate spiritual formation among our readers.

ISBN 1-57683-382-8

Cover designed by Ray Moore
Cover photo by Veer
Creative Team: Terry Behimer, Don Simpson, Amy Spencer, Glynese Northam

Some of the anecdotal illustrations in this book are true to life and are included with the permission of the persons involved. All other illustrations are composites of real situations, and any resemblance to people living or dead is coincidental.

Unless otherwise identified, all Scripture quotations in this publication are taken from the HOLY BIBLE: NEW INTERNATIONAL VERSION® (NIV®). Copyright © 1973, 1978, 1984 by International Bible Society. Used by permission of Zondervan Publishing House. All rights reserved. The other version used is the *New American Standard Bible* (NASB), © The Lockman Foundation 1960, 1962, 1963, 1968, 1971, 1972, 1973, 1975, 1977.

Egeler, Daniel, 1958-
  Mentoring millennials : shaping the next hero generation / Daniel Egeler.-- 1st ed.
    p. cm.
Includes bibliographical references.
  ISBN 1-57683-382-8 (pbk.)
  1. Mentoring in church work. I. Title.
BV4408.5.E37 2003
253'.7--dc21
                            2003004150

Printed in Canada

1 2 3 4 5 6 7 8 9 10 / 07 06 05 04 03

To my wife, Kathleen,
for her unswerving love, complete support, and encouragement.

To my children, Andrew, Danielle, Matthew, and Bethany,
for their sacrifice of time while Dad travels all over the world on
behalf of missionary kids and Christian education.

To my parents, Arnold and Dorothy,
who made the sacrifice to serve God on the continent of Africa and
have demonstrated uncompromising lives of holiness through their
years of ministry.

To my siblings, Timothy, Jonathon, James, and Ruth,
who shared in all of my joys and heartaches while growing up as
missionary kids in Africa.

To God be the glory.

Contents

ACKNOWLEDGMENTS   9

PREFACE   11

PART ONE: UNDERSTANDING MILLENNIALS

Chapter One   Leaving a Legacy   15
Chapter Two   The Millennial Generation: Good News
                 from the Front   25
Chapter Three   The Lost Children: Bad News from the Front   41
Chapter Four   The Full Spectrum: Living in the
                 Postmodern Era   53

PART TWO: EMPOWERING MILLENNIALS

Chapter Five   Understanding Mentoring   71
Chapter Six   Passive Mentoring   89
Chapter Seven   Occasional Mentoring   105
Chapter Eight   Intensive Mentoring   125
Chapter Nine   Mentoring Lessons: The Barnabas Model   139

NOTES   149

ABOUT THE AUTHOR   157

Acknowledgments

MANY PEOPLE HAVE CONTRIBUTED TO THE WRITING OF THIS BOOK. THE COM-munity that comprised the Alliance Academy in Quito, Ecuador, and the East African missionary community that surrounded me during my formative years demonstrated models of adult involvement in the lives of young people that served as a foundation for the premise of this book. You will find several stories of mentoring relationships from these communities included in the following chapters. There were, however, many more stories that could have been told. These were indeed special communities and, unfortunately, I sometimes took for granted the privilege of living with men and women committed to investing in the lives of young people.

Frank Hankins, a Christian & Missionary Alliance missionary in Ecuador, was instrumental in reaffirming the importance of mentoring in my ministry at the Alliance Academy. Frank also introduced me to the writing of Paul Stanley and Bobby Clinton, and it is their conceptual framework of the levels of mentoring that shapes the outline of this book.

I am grateful to Shelley Webb for starting the whole process by asking if I had ever considered writing a book after hearing me share some of my stories. I also owe a great debt of gratitude to Terry Behimer, who provided advice and counsel far beyond her professional responsibilities during those early days of writing, and to Don Simpson and Greg Clouse, who used their God-given gifts to assist me throughout the editing process.

Finally, my wife, Kathy, provided support and encouragement throughout the entire writing process by shouldering a larger-than-normal parenting burden. My children, Andrew, Danielle, Matthew, and Bethany, also sacrificed much of their time with Dad during their vacations while time was devoted to the writing of this book. My prayer is that this sacrifice was not in vain.

Preface

A PERSUASIVE ARGUMENT CAN BE MADE THAT WE'RE ON THE CUSP OF THE next "hero generation." The Millennials (young men and women born after 1982) are bursting onto the scene with enormous promise. They are surprisingly resourceful, and in many ways they seem to be like the "GI generation" of World War II, which Tom Brokaw has dubbed America's greatest.

But Millennials are entering a world of great challenge—heirs of the dot-com bust, corporate corruption, and the terror of 9-11. They seem destined to fight wars of their own to secure peace in the free world. At home, they sometimes grow up lonely and feeling left out. It's not that they're unwanted, but in the hustle and bustle of a two-income household in a consumer society, their parents typically have little time for them. What's more, this generation has had drilled into it the postmodern siren song that there is no such thing as absolute truth—indeed, that tolerance is the ultimate virtue.

So, how do we mentor this generation?

This has become clear: we mentor them with authenticity and love. Only the genuineness of a life that does what it says—the twin pistons of preaching *and* living the truth—will reach these young adults. The Millennial generation craves connection and authenticity, and responds to genuine love. As Jesus taught, "By this all men will know that you are my disciples, if you love one another" (John 13:35).

Are you a mentor?

In some way, every believer is a mentor. Because discipleship—or mentoring—is built into the DNA of Christian faith, the goal of every believer should be to hone his or her mentoring style to more intentionally and effectively connect with and invest in the lives of the next generation. In this way, the next generation will see Jesus in the fabric of our lives.

Mentoring Millennials is not a book about theory or a technical rendering of how to mentor. Instead, the heartbeat of this book is stories from the front. Mentoring is most effectively caught by example. The Millennial generation is most profoundly touched by authenticity and example, and I trust that these personal experiences will exude genuineness and the importance of a relational connection in action. If my stories are convincing, you will begin to incarnate their truth without necessarily being aware of the change that is taking place within you. At least I pray this will be your experience as you walk with me.

This book builds on the conceptual framework for mentoring proposed by Paul Stanley and Robert Clinton in *Connecting: The Mentoring Relationships You Need to Succeed in Life* (NavPress, 1992). I use their three-level model—passive mentoring, occasional mentoring, and intensive mentoring—to organize my storytelling.

I often quote this Chinese proverb:

> If you are planting for a year, plant grain.
> If you are planting for a decade, plant trees.
> If you are planting for a century, plant people.[1]

I challenge you to be about this business of planting people—for your investment will reap an eternal legacy.

P A R T   O N E

UNDERSTANDING

MILLENNIALS

CHAPTER ONE

Leaving a Legacy

THE 1968 OLYMPICS IN MEXICO CITY WERE THE FIRST SUMMER GAMES TO BE held at high altitude—7,400 feet above sea level. One of the United States' Olympic hopefuls that year was Jim Ryan. He was not only a world-record holder in the mile, but also a dedicated, outspoken Christian.

My family had returned to the United States from East Africa for a one-year missionary furlough, and we joined a large portion of our extended family in a relative's living room to watch the Olympic final for the 1,500 meters. Anticipation was running high, as it was a virtual certainty that the Stars and Stripes would be raised to honor Jim Ryan, the expected gold medal winner.

Indeed, Ryan quickly took the lead and soon was far ahead of the pack. The excitement in the living room was palpable. As the bell lap began, aunts, uncles, and cousins were on their feet cheering.

I squirmed to get a good look at the TV screen and noticed the lithe, last-place African runner suddenly surge forward at almost a sprinter's pace. By the time Ryan was cresting the final turn to sprint to the finish line, the African runner was right alongside him. As they raced shoulder to shoulder, the roar in the living room was deafening. Just before the finish line, the African runner outkicked Ryan to win the gold medal, and there was only one person in the living room still screaming—me. I didn't even realize it until I saw everyone's look of shock mixed with a tinge of anger. How could I be cheering against an American?

That's when it hit me like a ton of bricks—I was different from my red-white-and-blue American cousins. I had divided loyalties that spanned two continents. I (and my cousins) quickly realized I was pulling for the African runner. The winner of the 1500-meter race was Kip Keino—a Kenyan—the first of a long line of Kenyan Olympic gold medalists in the distance events.

Kenya is located in East Africa, the part of the world where I had grown up as a child of missionary parents. Kip was also a vibrant Christian who had been raised in a small village in the high altitude of the Great Rift Valley. As a child and young man, he had run everywhere, and this high-altitude training turned out to be a huge advantage when competing in the rarified air of Mexico City.

In their book *The Sacred Romance*, Brent Curtis and John Eldredge introduce a concept that they call "the message of the arrows."[1] These authors believe that there are only two things that pierce our hearts: beauty and affliction. Affliction (what they call "arrows") often brings with it a message, the most defining of which strikes our lives when we are young and our hearts are most vulnerable. My particular arrow from this experience was the pain of feeling different and left out. The accompanying messages were *"God must not really care about you if he sent your parents to Africa"; "Since you grew up in Africa, you'll always be different and isolated"; "Because you're different, there must be something wrong with you."* Due to these messages of the arrows, I decided to be very careful about exposing my loyalties or sharing my history, because I wanted to be accepted and to fit in.

The Kindness of Coach Bennett

Several years later, my parents returned to live in the United States permanently. I remember driving around our new hometown for the first time. We had moved to this community only because we had free housing for a year, thanks to a house-sitting opportunity. The streets were lined with beautiful maple trees and each house had a lush green lawn. It was obviously a wealthy neighborhood.

Being struck with the standard of living and knowing we were still living on a missionary income, I felt the burning in the pit of my stomach as all the past messages of the arrows reemerged. Questions and fears swarmed me from all sides: *Will I fit in here or am I going to be different? Do I have to be a "rich kid" to fit in? Should I risk letting these kids know that I grew up in East Africa? I wonder if I can make the varsity soccer team? I wonder if the coach will even give me a chance as a senior? Does God really care about how I feel?* As the thought of being excluded began to gnaw at me, I made a silent vow to bury my past, use my well-honed cross-cultural skills, and learn to become a "real" American.

My dad was pretty astute, and he realized I was apprehensive about this final year of high school (my third school in three years). He offered to take me to the high school to meet the soccer coach and to get the details on the varsity tryouts. As we pulled into the parking lot of the large red-brick high school, uncertainty again began to well up inside me. The receptionist doubted that the soccer coach would even be in, as it was still summer vacation, but she went ahead and dialed his extension. With a surprised look, she obviously had gotten a response. She hung up the phone and said, "Coach Bennett is in and he's looking forward to meeting you." She then took the time to draw a map of the twists and turns we would have to navigate to find his office. As we walked through the dark, silent halls, I prayed that this would be a positive meeting.

Once we arrived in the hallway by the gymnasium, I noticed a short, energetic man waiting outside an open door. When he saw us looking for an office, he quickly came our way and introduced himself. "Hi, I'm Coach Bennett, and you must be Dan." He had a twinkle in his eye, and I could tell he was genuinely interested in meeting me. I spent the next half-hour telling him about my background and learning about the soccer program and tryout schedule. Before we left, Coach Bennett told me the returning varsity players were holding an impromptu scrimmage in the city park that evening and invited me to attend.

When I showed up for the pickup game that evening, Coach Bennett was there to introduce me to the other players, and he stayed around to watch the scrimmage. I didn't realize it until later in the season, but that was the only time all summer he stopped by to watch the guys play.

The tryouts for the varsity soccer team were quite competitive—seventy-five athletes vying for eighteen roster slots. The school's soccer program was perennially ranked among the state's top twenty, had a large following in the student body and community, and received frequent press coverage. As we all gathered in the middle of the field, Coach Bennett thanked everyone for making the effort to try out for the team and informed us that the varsity roster would be posted on the bulletin board outside his office.

After three days of tryouts, I nervously got in line to check the soccer roster and watched as many young men left crestfallen and disappointed. I finally reached the front of the line and couldn't believe my eyes. I had made the team!

Inside the locker room, everyone else was whooping it up and celebrating. When the coach announced it was time to hand out jerseys, a mad scramble ensued. I couldn't figure out what was going on, so I ended up at the back of the line. Then I realized what was happening: each player was selecting his jersey number, and whoever was at the beginning of the line got his preference. This was completely foreign to me because, in the part of the world where I had lived, jersey numbers were assigned based on each player's position (if you wore the number 10, you were a forward; if you wore the number 3, you were a defender, and so on).

When I finally reached the window, Coach Bennett asked, "What number do you want, son?"

I looked around and shrugged my shoulders. "Since I'm the last one in line, I guess I'll take whatever is left." Coach's eyes twinkled and, with a smile, he said, "Here . . . I noticed you were the last in line and I've saved a jersey for you." He handed me a jersey with the number 5 and said, "This was the number I wore in high school and college. I want you to have it."

I was stunned and I felt my eyes well up with tears. I could hardly choke out a "thank you" as I took the jersey.

Sometimes God uses people to reveal the lie embedded in the messages of the arrows. Coach Bennett noticed me, included me, and made me feel special at a point when I was especially vulnerable and when the messages of the arrows were particularly appealing. I'm sure he did not understand the full ramifications of what had happened with that small act of kindness, but he impacted my life in a powerful way.

After my senior year, I became an "American" and fought to get in the front of every line for the privilege of selecting my soccer jersey.

And in every one of my subsequent soccer pictures, I'm wearing the number 5. In fact, dozens of young men around the world are now wearing the number 5, and the number has equal significance for them. Why? Because as a soccer coach, I would tell my team members the story of the number 5 and challenge them to accept the baton Coach Bennett handed to me, and then pass it on with their own acts of kindness. Perhaps they too will have the opportunity to change a life forever!

Upon graduating from high school, I attended a small Christian liberal arts college on an athletic and academic scholarship. It was during my college years that I had another life-changing experience with one of my teachers.

A Visit from Miss Jackson

Just as I was getting ready to leave my dorm room to answer the phone at the end of the hall, a classmate shouted, "Dan, the phone's for you!" I wondered who could be calling; it was mid-morning and I was getting a bit of studying done between classes. As I picked up the receiver, I recognized my father's voice.

"Someone you haven't seen for a long time is in town. It's your elementary school teacher, Miss Jackson, and she wants to catch up on your life. She'll be by to eat lunch with you in the cafeteria today."

Feeling an obligation to honor my father and my former teacher, I agreed to the invitation, but I was a bit worried about everyone seeing me with my primary school teacher. So I planned to get to lunch early, escort Miss Jackson through the line, and find a table in the corner of the cafeteria. Maybe no one would notice me eating with her.

Once we made connections an hour or so later, I walked slowly and deliberately to allow Miss Jackson to keep up with me. She walked as though in pain—I remembered how she had always seemed so strong and confident when she was teaching.

I had grown up on a remote island in Lake Victoria, the source of the Nile River in East Africa. The best schooling option for me was a one-room schoolhouse on the shores of the lake that offered a boarding program for elementary students. At the age of eight, I went to this school for the first time and Miss Jackson was my teacher. In fact, she was my teacher for virtually all of my elementary years. Miss Jackson spent her entire career in a corner of Africa teaching the children of missionaries—and I was one of her kids.

As Miss Jackson addressed me ("Daniel") from across the lunch table, I immediately felt the urge to sit up straight and pay attention. Her voice had not changed; it still commanded respect. We talked about our memories and my life at college. As we neared the end of the conversation, Miss Jackson paused as if deep in thought. She reached down into her purse and pulled out a worn, faded, black notebook. Flipping through the pages, she paused periodically and read out the name of a classmate and told me what that person was doing these days. In nearly every case, she ended her update with a summary of how she envisioned they would invest their lives for eternity.

Finally, Miss Jackson pulled out her pen and opened the faded notebook to a fresh, blank page. She carefully wrote my name at the top and slowly jotted down some of the key points of our conversation. Then she paused, looked straight at me, and said, "Daniel (I sat up straight), now I want to know how you're going to invest *your* life for eternity." I was speechless. And because of that, I felt embarrassed and ashamed.

By this point in my life, thanks to Coach Bennett's influence, I was no longer ashamed of my heritage. However, I had succumbed to a new and potentially more destructive message of the arrow, deciding that I would not make the same mistake my dad and Miss Jackson had made. From my perspective, they had gotten stuck in some little corner of Africa and no one knew who they were. That would never be me. My main objective was to make a name for myself and leave my imprint on the world. People were going to know Dan Egeler.

As I got ready for bed that night, the conviction of the Holy Spirit pierced my heart. I realized all that Miss Jackson had given up. She had never married. The loneliness must have been crushing during the quiet African nights and during the holidays when she was apart from her family. She must have doubted the validity and cost of her commitment when the years began to mount. Miss Jackson never achieved tenure or received professional recognition for her achievements—and those were remarkable. Yet she taught the span of five grades in a multigrade one-room schoolhouse and was able to fan the flame of a love of lifelong learning in each student. That's the definition of "master teacher"!

Miss Jackson never was able to contribute to a 401(k) and build up a healthy nest egg. Instead, she invested in the lives of young children whose parents were so committed to the Great Commission that they were willing to sacrifice the comforts of their own culture to venture to another. When Miss Jackson arrives at the judgment seat, she'll hear the voice of her Savior saying, "Well done, good and faithful servant," and for the rest of eternity she'll have a line of more than a hundred missionary kids queuing up to embrace her and thank her for her efforts on their behalf.

I knelt down beside my bed that night and made a new vow: to refute the message of the arrows and commit to redefining success based on an eternal perspective. A few years later, I heard the bittersweet news that Miss Jackson had gone on to heaven. It was then I truly realized her intention of passing the baton from one generation to another. This baton was the commitment to live in light of eternity. It was Miss Jackson's legacy, and now the challenge was to make it mine.

Teachers Turned Mentors

As you may have guessed by now, based on the topic of this book, I consider both Miss Jackson and Coach Bennett my mentors.

Miss Jackson devoted her entire professional career to investing in the lives of missionary kids like me. It was a tremendous sacrifice, but one that she willingly made in obedience to the King of kings. She cemented that legacy by crisscrossing the country to challenge her past students to live their lives "in light of eternity." Great will be her reward in heaven.

Likewise, Coach Bennett invested in my life with one small act of kindness. At that moment, he and I never realized the total significance of this display of caring. But it shaped me forever.

The lesson is that each of us can be a mentor. The role doesn't necessarily entail spending your life in Africa or even as a full-time teacher or coach—it may just take a small act of kindness that the Holy Spirit can turn into a powerful force in the life of a young person. Such is the hallmark of a mentor.

CHAPTER TWO

The Millennial Generation:

Good News from the Front

A CANADIAN-BORN MILLENNIAL, CRAIG KIELBURGER, IS A WONDERFUL EXAM-
ple of the hope and promise of this generation of young people. When
he was twelve, Craig read a *Toronto Star* article about a twelve-year-
old Pakistani, sold into bondage as a carpet weaver, who dared to
speak out against child labor—and then was murdered.[1] Craig's life
was altered forever after reading that story. Within five years, Craig
(now seventeen) and his friends had succeeded in establishing Free
the Children, a global youth network with a hundred thousand volunteers in more than twenty countries.

Using the Internet and working closely with a variety of public
and private organizations, Craig's group helped build child-worker
rehabilitation sites in Asia, set up job cooperatives for mothers of
Latin American child workers (enabling the latter to go to school),
created rescue homes for Middle Eastern camel jockeys, extracted
Filipino children from the sex trade, and organized a European boy-
cott of carpets that lack a "rug mark" guaranteeing they are not made
by children. Their volunteers aided hurricane relief in Nicaragua, sent
health kits and baby items to Kosovo, campaigned to get the police to
assist Mexico's child beggars, and sought to criminalize "child sex

tourism." Free the Children's new goal is to mobilize teens across the globe to get their governments to ban all forms of child labor and criminally punish those responsible.[2] Now, that's an example of a Millennial maximizing his potential!

The unfortunate truth is that we rarely hear the good news about the Craig Kielburgers of our world. Indeed, the bad news of today's generation of young people seems to have captured the attention of the media. For example, consider the March 15-17, 2002, *USA Today* cover article entitled "The Sexual Revolution Hits Junior High." The article was replete with anecdotal evidence from educators, parents, and other experts reporting that sexual activity among today's young people was beginning much earlier than with past generations. The core data cited was a survey conducted by a Washington research group indicating an increase from 11 percent to 19 percent (between 1988 and 1995) in females who said they had had sex before the age of fourteen.[3]

For boys, however, the numbers did not increase at all. Furthermore, deep into the article, the authors acknowledged that experts can't make hard conclusions until they can get "good, current numbers on nationwide trends." One expert simply stated, "It could be getting worse, it could be getting better, we just don't know."[4] The reliable data contained in the article certainly did not seem to warrant the corresponding headline. Sadly, the downside to this drumbeat of negativity is that it tends to shape our perspective on today's youth culture. As such, most adults would probably concur that this next generation is headed down the wrong path.

While certainly there is some legitimate bad news relating to today's youth (the aforementioned article gave plenty of sobering statistics), there also is some good news—and it's news we need to hear.

A Good News Revolution

In their book *Millennials Rising: The Next Great Generation,* Neil Howe and William Strauss profiled this current generation in light of earlier generations, including the GI generation (born between 1901 and 1924), the Silent generation (born between 1925 and 1942), the Boomer generation (born between 1943 and 1960), and the Xer generation (born between 1961 and 1981). The authors call the current generation the Millennials, those young people born since 1982 whose parents are part of the Boomer generation.[5] Much of the research Howe and Strauss have conducted contrasts the attitudes and behaviors that characterized the coming of age for Boomers (the parents) with that of the Millennials (the kids). They contend that the Millennial generation is running completely counter to past trends — and the Millennial trend is definitely a positive one.

Howe and Strauss go on to state,

> There's a revolution under way among today's kids — a good news revolution. This generation is going to rebel by behaving not worse, but better. Their life mission will not be to tear down old institutions that don't work, but to build up new ones that do. Look closely at youth indicators, and you'll see that Millennial attitudes and behaviors represent a sharp break from Generation X, and are running exactly counter to trends launched by the Boomers. Across the board, Millennial kids are challenging a long list of common assumptions about what "postmodern" young people are supposed to become.[6]

A significant factor that seems to have contributed to the Millennials' positive attitudes and behaviors is that this is a generation of children born in an age in which they are much more wanted by the adult society around them. The Boomers obviously felt a desire to bear and raise children. This desire first was demonstrated with a quadrupling in the number of infertility-related doctor visits from 1986 to 1988 and then, second, with the rising birthrate.[7] The result was the "echo boomlet."

The rising birth rate was a tremendous surprise to demographers, who did not anticipate this change in the national perception toward children. Once the national birth rate leveled off at about 3.6 million between 1980 and 1983, it didn't start to drift down. Instead, the birth rate rose again, to 3.8 million in 1987, 4 million in 1989, and 4.2 million in 1990. By the late 1990s, the annual number of births had stabilized at around 3.9 million—roughly 20 percent higher than the mid-'70s rate.[8] Clearly, Boomers viewed children not as a hindrance, but as a blessing.

It appears the adult investment in this Millennial generation has borne fruit. A persuasive argument can be made that we're on the cusp of the next hero generation. The last hero generation was the GI generation that confronted the evils of Nazi Germany and prevailed with great sacrifice. Authors Howe and Strauss argue that

> having been proclaimed by Tom Brokaw as America's
> "greatest generation," the GI Generation is passing
> away gradually to fond memories. Many of those
> memories call to mind a generation of mythic
> heroism and civic grandeur—of the Americans who
> pulled the nation out of the Great Depression,

conquered half the globe as wartime soldiers,
unleashed nuclear power, founded suburbia, took
mankind to the moon, and laid the cornerstones for
a "Great Society" that their more self-absorbed off-
spring were unable or unwilling to complete.[9]

Ironically, the GI generation's most important link to the Millennials could be in the void they leave behind. With the departure of what author Robert Putnam calls "America's long civic generation,"[10] no other adult peer group possesses anything close to their upbeat, high-achieving, team-playing, and civic-minded reputation. There is a growing realization that today's parents have sensed this void and have focused on teaching these GI values to their Millennial children. As a result, these kids seem to be gravitating toward the GI generation as their generational role models.[11] Certainly, they hold this generation in much higher esteem than they hold all the other past generations.

Howe and Strauss conducted their own independent research in Fairfax County, Virginia, with the graduating class of 2000 (the first Millennial generation class to graduate from high school). According to the results, nearly all of the high school seniors surveyed thought of the GI or World War II generation as a synonym for "grandparent." This perception is interesting, because for most Millennials, GIs are in fact their great-grandparents. More importantly, these Millennials associated the word "hero" more readily with people in their eighties (the GI generation) than with people in any other age bracket. By a whopping five-to-one margin, these students believed that this elder generation had a "mainly positive" reputation—a much greater "pos-itive" margin than they gave to any other generation.[12]

The Analogy of the Linchpin

With the Millennials' obvious affinity to the last hero generation, the question is, How can adults reinforce this positive link between generations and thus maximize the potential of the Millennial generation?

In his book *Mentoring: Confidence in Finding a Mentor and Becoming One,* Bobb Biehl uses the analogy of a linchpin to illustrate the importance of connecting one generation to another. A linchpin is a small piece of metal used to connect a tractor to a trailer. It's not very expensive, and it's not very elaborate, but it's crucial. As Biehl states,

> Basically, a linchpin is a single piece of steel that is not very large but is very important because with it, the powerful doodlebug (or tractor) can pull a wagon that is hundreds or even thousands of times heavier than the linchpin. . . . In this simple analogy, the doodlebug is the current generation of Christian leadership. It has a lot of power, but it needs to bring the next generation of leadership (the loaded wagon) along in the process of moving through history. The linchpin of Christian leadership development is the mentoring process.[13]

The process of mentoring is the linchpin to connect one generation to another. It's not very elaborate, and it doesn't take a rocket scientist to figure out, but it's crucial in making the connection between generations. Howe and Strauss propose, "The next quarter century will reveal whether a 'need or opportunity' will in fact arise for Millennials, a hero trial that could reveal a 'capacity for greatness' commensurate with what Americans revere in hero generations of the past."[14] Given the fact that Howe and Strauss wrote this *before* the events of September 11, 2001, could it be that this next generation will be the one to confront and prevail over the evil of religious terrorism? Fifty years from now, will historians be writing about the Millennials as another great hero generation based on their response to this challenge?

Barbara Kantrowitz and Keith Naughton wrote a thought-provoking essay in *Newsweek* that supported the idea that September 11 would provide great opportunity for the Millennial generation. The authors maintained that this Millennial generation that "once had it all—peace, prosperity, even the dot-com dream of retiring at 30—faces its defining moment."[15] Greg Epstein, a graduate student in Judaic studies at the University of Michigan, was quoted in the article as saying,

> Our generation, as long as we've had an identity, was known as the generation that had it easy. We had no crisis, no Vietnam, no Martin Luther King, no JFK. We've got it now. When we have kids and grandkids, we'll tell them that we lived through the roaring '90s, when all we cared about was the No. 1 movie or how many copies an album sold. This is where it changes.[16]

Perhaps Epstein is right. Perhaps Howe, Strauss, and others are also correct in suggesting that this Millennial generation has the potential to be the next hero generation. If so, then anyone interested in making an eternal impact on the next generation should become very excited.

A Close-up of the Millennials

As today's adults attempt to authentically connect to the Millennial generation, it's helpful to understand the attitudes and behaviors of these young men and women. The preponderance of the evidence seems to indicate that the Millennial generation's behavior and attitudes are significantly different from those of its Boomer and Xer predecessors. This attitude shift is particularly noticeable in terms of this generation's (1) optimism, (2) achievement orientation, (3) desire for rules and boundaries, (4) acceptance of authority with a corresponding support of traditional values, and (5) desire to commit to a cause.

A number of surveys show that, compared to Xer and Boomer teens, Millennial teens are much more optimistic about the world in which they're growing up. Nine in ten describe themselves as "happy," "confident," and "positive."[17] This is a significant departure from the pessimistic outlook on life that Xers and Boomers had at that age. The Millennials' optimistic outlook is further supported by the hard data that teen suicide rates are now falling for the first time in decades.[18]

Another significant departure from previous generations is the Millennials' healthy attitude toward school. Eight in ten teenagers say it's "cool to be smart" (as opposed to past generations, who considered academic achievers to be "geeks"). This positive peer pressure that supports academic excellence is critical for educators who work to develop a positive learning environment in schools.

A record share of teenagers are taking Advanced Placement (AP) tests, and these students say they "look forward to school" and plan to attend college.[19] Compared to students in the late '80s, today's Millennial seniors are nearly three times as likely to take calculus, are twice as likely to take all three major sciences (biology, chemistry, physics), and are taking twice as many AP tests. The number of high school graduates who attend college the semester after they graduate has risen from 50 percent among Boomers in 1975, to 60 percent among Gen Xers in 1990, to 65 percent among Millennials in 1996.[20]

Educators are also noticing that this generation of teens appears more desirous of order, rules, and clear boundaries for behavior. The Millennials' preference for boundaries exhibits itself in their dislike for any lack of order in their classrooms. When public school students are asked what they would like addressed in their schools, a majority of them mention "good manners," "maintaining discipline in the classroom," and making kids "treat each other with respect." Furthermore, 40 percent of those surveyed said unruly student behavior interfered with their schoolwork.[21] Educators used to work against peer pressure because it was usually tied to breaking the rules—which was once considered to be "cool." Now educators are trying to harness positive peer pressure through the use of student juries, peer grading, and other educational strategies to support adherence to rules and structure.[22]

Beyond just desiring more order, Millennials appear to be concerned about the state of moral and social values within their society. The Horatio Alger Association of Distinguished Americans conducted a 1996 survey that demonstrated that the most significant concern among Millennials was the decline in moral and social values.[23] In the 1995–1996 edition of *Who's Who Among American High School Students,* teenagers listed the same concern, the first time such a response had been given in the history of the publication.[24]

Another strong indication of the Millennial generation's apparent return to morality is reflected in a decline in the percentage of teens engaging in sexual activity, for the first time in twenty-five years.

According to the National Survey of Family Growth, the percentage of teenage girls participating in sex rose from 29 percent in 1970 to 55 percent in 1990, but had dropped to 50 percent in 1997.[25] The research of Barbara Risman and Pepper Schwartz, specialists with the Council on Contemporary Families, also indicates this positive trend, reporting that the percentage of teens ages fifteen to seventeen who have had intercourse dropped from 54.1 in 1991 to 48.4 in 1997. Furthermore, they report that teen pregnancy rates dropped 17 percent from 1990 to 1996, and teen abortion rates dropped 16 percent from 1990 to 1995.[26]

This data is particularly interesting in that it runs directly counter to the *USA Today* article cited earlier in this chapter. In part, this discrepancy demonstrates that it's very difficult to get accurate data regarding youth perceptions. The important point, however, is that the *good news* from many of these surveys is seldom reported.

The Millennial generation also appears to embrace traditional values of home, family, and community. A major 1998 survey report summarized one of the most important new trends in youth opinion by pointing out that today's teens are rejecting the "too cool to care" credo of Generation X. Millennials do care; they are optimistic; and they embrace traditional values of home, family life, community, and education.[27]

Millennials Versus Boomers

Each generation tends to rebel in its own unique way. The Boomer generation reacted against what they considered the GI excesses of too much optimism, rationalism, and group-mindedness, and attempted to correct these excesses by turning toward rage, spiritualism, and self. Far from regarding GIs as the "greatest generation ever," Boomers were more likely to condemn GIs as America's worst generation and to protest against the establishment by throwing pig's blood at their institutional walls.

So how do the attitudes of Millennials compare to the Boomer generation, the generation of their parents? It seems that whereas Boomer children felt hemmed in by norms and rules, and came of age by assaulting them, Millennials show signs of trying to invite them back. Whereas Boomer teens had trouble talking to their parents (a major cause of the late-'60s "generation gap"), Millennials report a much better communication flow with their parents.[28] Whereas Boomers fought with their parents over values, Millennials seem to be willing to accept their parents' values.

Perhaps the biggest difference between today's teens and their Boomer parents is that Millennials think their generation will do a better job of collectively embodying these values. When asked whether "values and character" will matter more or less to their own generation when they're parents, they answer "more" by a two-to-one margin.[29] Indeed, when it comes to traditional values, Millennials hear their parents talk the good talk, but they themselves aren't satisfied with mere symbol and gesture. They intend to be authentic and walk the walk.

A Spiritual Ripeness

The Millennial desire for authenticity is borne out in their perception of religion. In a *Newsweek* article (May 8, 2000), author John Leland pointed out that "the unsung story of today's teenagers may be how religious they are."[30] Indeed, in an earlier *Newsweek* poll, 78 percent of teenagers said that religion is important, and many gladly identified themselves as "spiritual," though few wanted to be labeled as "religious."[31]

Christian pollster George Barna notes that two out of three teens strongly desire a personal relationship with God. The downside, according to Barna, is that fewer than half are excited about church, which has left many church leaders wondering how to reach this complicated generation.[32] One of the key reasons that more than half of Millennials are not excited about church is due to the perceived hypocrisy they see in the adult religious community.

In an article written for *Christianity Today*, author Wendy Murray Zoba persuasively argued that two defining characteristics of the Millennial generation are that they're activists and that they long for God.[33] When this generation commits to a belief or a cause, they commit with passion and vigor. But the focus of their passion needs to be something that is authentic and genuine.

In Murray Zoba's book *Generation 2K: What Parents and Others Need to Know About the Millennials,* she says this intense desire to commit to an authentic and meaningful cause stems from a propensity to live "in the extreme."

> Moral ambiguity has spurred [Millennials] to want
> decisive boundaries and real answers. Spiritual
> longing has made them ready to give it everything
> they've got in their quest for God. In other words,
> they will do things in the extreme. When they
> answer the call to heroism, they will answer it

boldly. When it comes to embracing moral truth, they will do so unabashedly. When they give their lives to the Lord, they will serve with everything on the line.[34]

Murray Zoba feels that the time is right for parents and the church to seize this season of spiritual ripeness in young people, to capture their longings, win their allegiance, and equip them to give it everything they've got to carry the "extreme gospel" into the coming decades.[35]

Sharing Murray Zoba's perspective, Christian recording artist and author Rebecca St. James connects with today's teens by going beyond the salvation presentation. She believes Jesus can save but he also wants everything you've got.[36] This message of total commitment really resonates with the Millennial generation.

Giving Themselves for a Worthy Cause

Millennials go beyond just *desiring* to commit to a cause; they are much more prone to voluntarily contribute their time toward what they feel are worthy endeavors. The Independent Sector, an organization that tracks nonprofit activities, conducted a 1996 study which indicated that in 1995, 13.3 million young people between the ages of twelve and seventeen spent 2.4 billion hours volunteering. That is a 7-percent rise in the number of teens volunteering and a 17-percent increase over the number of hours donated in 1991.[37]

It seems that a new Millennial service ethic is emerging, built around notions of teamwork, support for civic institutions, and participation in good deeds. The story of Craig Kielburger at the beginning of this chapter is not an anomaly. Surveys show that five of every six Millennials believe their generation has the greatest duty to improve the environment. At a rate far higher than that of the adult generations, Millennials would impose extra civic duties on themselves, including taxes, to achieve results.[38] Interestingly, adults give a higher priority to helping kids do good deeds than to doing good deeds themselves. On average, middle-aged Boomers spend fewer hours doing community service than do Millennial teens.[39]

Rendezvous with Destiny

"To some generations, much is given. Of other generations, much is expected. This generation has a rendezvous with destiny."[40] So said Franklin Delano Roosevelt while accepting the nomination for his second term as president in 1936. He was speaking to the coming-of-age GI generation, whose "rendezvous with destiny" came at a time when they faced an economic depression at home and the rising possibility of war abroad.

As mentioned earlier in the chapter, when we consider the events of September 11, could the coming-of-age Millennial generation be keeping another rendezvous with destiny? Could the Millennials discover that they are in fact the next generation from whom "much is expected"? And will they respond in hero fashion? It appears that the trial has already arrived on their doorstep—whether its members wish it or not.

In their *Newsweek* article entitled "Generation 9-11," Barbara Kantrowitz and Keith Naughton argue that the Millennials are uniquely positioned to understand and respond to the "hero trial" of the clash of cultures that culminated in 9-11. While the high school history lessons of past generations concentrated almost exclusively on Western Europe, the Millennials have learned about Chinese dynasties, African art, Islam. This generation is much more likely to have friends from many economic and ethnic backgrounds, given the demographic diversity of their campuses.[41] As Judith Rodin, the president of the University of Pennsylvania, concluded, "I think they realize more than the adults that this is a clash of cultures, something we haven't seen in a thousand years."[42]

Our Call

Jerry Wunder, vice president of China operations for Mission Training International, tells a story of helping his daughter set up for a track race in the high hurdles.[43] She attended a small private school that occasionally had to scrounge around to come up with enough equipment to outfit the athletics program. For this particular race, Jerry's daughter asked if he could help her hold the starting blocks, because the school didn't have the proper equipment needed to hold them in place. Jerry immediately agreed to the task. He had been doing quite a bit of traveling and this was one of his rare opportunities to watch his daughter perform.

Before the race began, Jerry carefully knelt down behind his daughter and tightly gripped each block as the starter raised his pistol. Jerry knew that his daughter often won her races by starting quickly and establishing an early lead, so he keenly felt his responsibility. The starter's pistol sounded, and his daughter got out to a fabulous start. As she rounded the first turn, it appeared that she was in the lead, but as she headed into the straightaway, he couldn't see her progress because people were blocking his view. He tried to jump up in the air to catch a glimpse of the finish but his effort was futile. What a disappointment—he finally had a chance to watch his daughter compete, but he did not see the end of the race.

Isn't that a perfect illustration of how life works when it comes to evaluating each generation's impact and the fulfillment of its destiny? As we pass the baton to the Millennials, seeking to instill an eternal perspective into their hearts, we don't know how the race is going to end. We may jump up and down, hoping to catch a glimpse, but we're just not going to see the final result. Nevertheless, we must faithfully and carefully lay the groundwork for their success by holding the starting blocks (being there, helping them realize their capabilities, directing their fervor) and using the linchpin of mentoring to bring them along, all the time leaving the results to God. Of course, it will be up to the next generation to take the baton and run the race of their lives.

For all the promise of the Millennial generation, it is still very much a generation at risk—as the next chapter will most certainly demonstrate.

CHAPTER THREE

The Lost Children:
Bad News from the Front

You don't have to read too many Bible stories or biographies to realize that heroes aren't perfect people from perfect homes with perfect life circumstances. Many Millennials face a daunting uphill climb to reach their incredible potential. Even if the vast majority of our youngest generation is part of the "good news revolution" and the overall trends are positive, it's heartbreaking to come across real stories that truthfully share the stark images of a childhood without hope. And even one child without hope is one too many.

Several years ago, *Frontline*, a Public Broadcasting Service television program, produced a documentary on lonely kids so desperate to belong that they became deeply involved in a secret world of sex and its terrible consequences. These were young teenagers from affluent families, whose parents loved them and were able to provide them with good schools, big houses, and name-brand clothes to wear. Yet despite many advantages, these children in suburban Rockdale County, Georgia, unknowingly had unleashed a syphilis outbreak. With the news of this shocking development, a *Frontline* team spent more than five months interviewing teenagers, parents, schoolteachers, and administrators in Conyers, a town of about ten thousand people twenty miles southeast of Atlanta.

In the spring of 1996, an article appeared in the Conyers newspaper that revealed something was happening within the youth culture that up until then had been a complete mystery to the adult community. The article reported an outbreak of syphilis in town and hinted that there could be further cases in the future. The real shocking news, however, was that most of the cases involved middle-class teenage girls. As state health officials uncovered most of the cases and provided treatment, they also uncovered an underworld of teenage sex that involved multiple partners and what was termed "extreme" sexual activity.

In the end, seventeen teenagers tested positive for syphilis, two hundred others who had been exposed were treated, and it was discovered that more than fifty teenagers had engaged in extreme sex. What made this so frightening was that this was a population of teenagers who were not runaways or prostitutes—they came from suburban homes.

The Stories of Rockdale County

"DJ" was one of the more popular kids in his school, a boy everyone wanted to associate with. His parents were divorced, his father was wealthy, and he had little or no parental supervision. DJ stated that the sexual activity among the teens was "more of an underground railroad thing. Everybody was secretly having sex with everybody, and everybody knew it. The teenagers knew it. But the parents never knew."[1]

Another student, Nicole, simply stated that her friends' parents "cared what went on, but if it interfered with their lives they didn't really—wouldn't—they didn't want to bother with it."[2]

Peggy Cooper, a now-retired middle school guidance counselor in the district, characterized the common family dynamic as both parents working very hard to maintain a comfortable lifestyle, but with little to no involvement in the lives of their children. Cooper went on to describe how these kids were aching for attention. She said, "Children, when they come into this world, want attention, and they'll take good attention as long as they can get it. If they can't get good attention, they'll get bad attention because the worst thing in the world to them is to have no attention. No attention is to lead a solitary life."[3]

The lack of adult involvement in the kids' lives was not only evident in the teenagers' need for attention but in their active participation in deviant behavior without anyone to step in and provide cautionary guidance and direction. One of the investigators, Professor Claire Sterk of Emory University's School of Public Health, stated, "One of the things that was interesting about this group was that there was not necessarily a clearly defined leader. There was nobody around who fulfilled that role. So nobody stepped in, and the group kind of kept moving on without having anybody around who could pull the brake."[4]

The regrets expressed by the teenagers throughout the documentary are both haunting and heartbreaking. Many openly expressed regret at losing their virginity and at being too young to have had their first sexual experience. One young girl made a gut-wrenching comment when she said, "Staying a virgin until marriage is real good—I wish I could have done that."[5] One cannot watch without asking, "Where were the adults in these kids' lives?"

When Dr. Kathleen Toomey, director of the Georgia Division of Public Health, was brought in to speak to the community, she was stunned to see the depth of denial among the adults:

What was so extraordinary to me is these parents started looking externally for who to blame. "This has caused this," "TV has caused that," "External groups have caused this." But . . . none of them that I can recall ever looked to themselves. The minister turned to me and said, "They don't see. It's them. It's the parents. They have done this. The kids don't talk to them."[6]

In the end, the syphilis outbreak slipped off of everyone's radar screen. Some felt that the community—by treating the outbreak as an anomaly—had missed a larger point about all of its kids. Professor Sterk stated, "I would say it's very sad because there are so many lessons we could have learned from this. And part of me feels that we're not picking up on all those lessons and still leave adolescents hanging there, forcing them to take care of themselves when they're not always able to do that."[7]

Beth Ross, director of counseling for the Rockdale County Schools, lent support to this perspective by commenting,

I think there are a lot of children who are running their own lives, who really are testing limits or don't know what the limits are. They're like a balloon, out there floating around in the sky with little direction. And to run into a power line or to a tree and just burst is something they're very unaware that could happen. They don't know what's down the road. . . . Nobody has ever sat down and explained the limits to them.[8]

Wes Bonner, a youth pastor in Rockdale County, commented, "They have so many things, you know, every convenience. They all have a cell phone, a pager, anything that they need. But what they're looking for is, 'Where's the road? Where's the path?'"[9]

Throughout the documentary, one is repeatedly struck by the incredible longing that this generation has for connection and relationships. Rachel Dretzin Goodman, the wife in the husband-and-wife team who produced the documentary, was especially impacted by the kids' widespread loneliness and their longing for meaning and structure. She said, "We were struck by how widespread the kind of anomie, and loneliness, and hunger for structure and experimentation was, among kids all over the community."[10] It seemed that the parents and adults in the community were just too busy and self-absorbed to provide boundaries or to just be there to listen.

Later, in an article in *Christianity Today* that profiled the children of Rockdale County, Paula Rinehart provided a clear challenge for the Boomer generation of adults and parents when she wrote, "Against this dark backdrop of moral chaos, the radical hope of experiencing the transforming work of Christ shines like a diamond on black velvet. For Christians, this could be our best opportunity to speak life boldly to this generation."[11]

And a Thousand Miles Away in New England

In a 2002 *Atlantic Monthly* article entitled "The Apocalypse of Adolescence," Ron Powers wrote about the plight of youth in the bucolic state of Vermont. The author maintained that kids are in trouble in Vermont and the reasons are not easy to provide. In supporting his thesis, Powers pointed to the explosion in serious juvenile crime, the increase in the number of dropouts in the state's public schools, the increase in heroin abuse, and the prevalence of youth gangs.[12]

Chris Frappier, an investigator with the Vermont public defender's office, theorized that the youth gangs meet a need with these troubled teenagers:

> There's good within the gangs. They take care of each other. . . . So our kids, our children, who feel lost, disenfranchised—they join up! And why not! . . . What I'm seeing in recent years is the total and complete alienation of youth. And it's not coming from them; it's coming from the adults who aren't bothering to reach out to them. And it is terrifying.[13]

Powers concluded his article with this recommendation: a key to addressing this alienation of the youth—not just in Vermont but everywhere—is to "embrace an ethic of sustained mentoring that extends from community to personal relationships."[14]

Entering the World of Young Adults

Author Josh McDowell, a well-known Christian apologist who speaks to thousands of young people worldwide each year, hears them talk about an increasing sense of isolation. He maintains that this current generation of young people needs "strong relational connections" with adults in order to escape the loneliness that can pull them toward self-destruction. McDowell argues that it's almost impossible to pass on the previous generation's faith or values in this postmodern culture unless the adult generations make that "relational connection" with the younger generation.[15]

Too often, McDowell argues, adults tend to teach the truth by rules, regulations, and instruction. The problem is that these alone won't achieve the purpose—not without an emotional bond. Once this emotional bond is established, then the rules, regulations, and instruction will have context and meaning so that true learning can take place. McDowell concludes by saying,

> So, if we are going to pass on our values and our faith to our kids, we must do it in an "up-close and personal" manner. We can't instruct from a distance; we must enter their world and relate to them. I'm not talking about trying to live like teenagers—dressing like them, talking like them, listening to their music, etc. By entering their world, I mean being aware of what is happening in their lives and being there to make the appropriate relational connection.[16]

What McDowell is describing here is the process of mentoring. Research on schools showed interesting data regarding those schools that exhibited a high rate of retention (students staying in school). The average adult would assume teenagers would want to stay in school because of their relationships with their friends. However, the number-one variable that led to high student retention and contributed to a stable learning environment was the relationship of the adult staff to the students.[17]

I've found this to be true in my twenty-plus years as an educator. In fact, as a high school principal, I would pass on this lesson to my young teachers every year by urging them to avoid one particularly common pitfall: trying to become just another friend to their students. The truth is that most students already had enough friends. *What they didn't have were enough adults in their lives.* Despite the cues that often came across initially, the vast majority of kids would respect a teacher much more if he or she demonstrated genuine, authentic caring and concern *and* took the initiative to be an adult in their lives by providing boundaries, guidance, and direction.

Beth Ross, quoted earlier in this chapter, points out that adult guidance and the provision of boundaries and direction is critical for the emotional stability and happiness of young people:

> I think that there are a lot of children who aren't very happy. I think that most counselors will tell you the same thing: that children do need limits and they would feel better about themselves [if they had them]. They would have more confidence; they would have more direction. . . . They can't have direction unless they have some structure and some guidance from those who've been there and done that. . . . Whenever . . . they start doing things that are really inappropriate and could have significantly negative consequences . . . that's the time when parents and teachers and

other adults need to understand that the child is looking for limits.[18]

Providing Boundaries

Bill O'Reilly, host of Fox television network's *O'Reilly Factor,* did a program entitled "The Corruption of the American Child," in which he zeroed in on the challenges of growing up in American society. One segment of the special lent support to the idea that kids need adults in their lives, particularly adults who have the courage to provide boundaries.

One of O'Reilly's interviewees, child psychologist Dan Kindlon, commented on the difficulty parents have with setting boundaries for their Millennial kids. He attributed this to Boomer parents being "the generation that worshipped youth, that didn't trust authority, and to be that authority figure with kids can be difficult."[19] He went on to say that parents can make the mistake of thinking that you can't be friends with your child and strict at the same time.

Michael Josephson, a youth ethicist, used the illustration of cheating in school to highlight the danger laden in not confronting wrong behavior or providing boundaries and consequences. He maintained that almost 70 percent of kids today cheat in school. These kids hardly ever get caught, and when they do, they don't get punished. He said, "If you allow them to do the wrong thing without consequences, you confuse them as to right and wrong."[20]

O'Reilly concluded that many adults want to be their kids' peers rather than their parents. Being an adult in a teenager's life entails being willing to say what he or she may not want to hear—that's the difference between just being another friend and being an adult. However, if the adult has made that relational connection and is willing to provide authentic, loving guidance and direction, he or she will have fulfilled that teenager's deepest yearning.

A Memory from Overseas

The memory of one particular incident among the rash of school shootings that occurred in the late 1990s has remained with me. I was overseas at the time, and the foreign press had a strong fascination with this phenomenon of kids shooting kids in schools in the United States. In this case, reporters were translating an interview conducted with the high school principal, lauded as a hero for having coaxed a teenage boy into dropping his gun before anyone was seriously hurt. Because I understood English, I was able to listen in to the original context of the interview—and I'll never forget what was said.

The principal related how he came upon the young gunman at the end of a hallway; the boy was shaking with emotion. The principal slowly and calmly coaxed the teenager to lay the gun down on the ground and step forward. As the trembling boy slowly obeyed, the principal wrapped his arms around him in a hug. Holding the frightened, lonely boy in his embrace, he leaned forward and whispered in his ear, "What's your name, son?" He did not even know the boy's name!

Likely this was a young man who was lost in the cracks and had no significant adult in his life who could provide loving, caring guidance and correction when he needed it most. The principal was a hero, and justifiably so, but he had an impossible job. He was the chief administrator of a school of thousands and he could not be expected to know every student by name. And the size of his school could only have exacerbated the overwhelming loneliness and hopelessness this young man surely must have felt.

Making Time for Our Children

In her book *Generation 2K: What Parents and Others Need to Know About the Millennials,* Wendy Murray Zoba wrote of a successful mentoring program for Millennials implemented by Wayne Rice at Shadow Mountain Community Church in El Cajon, California. What is important to understand, said Rice, is that "our kids don't have any significant adults in their lives; some of them don't even have parents." He said that successful mentoring can be a struggle because "most people are too busy and don't have time for other people's kids. But that is why our kids are in trouble today. No one has time for them anymore."[21]

Professor Sterk would concur. In her interview for the *Frontline* documentary, she stated,

> I think adolescence has changed a lot over the last
> few decades. We expect a lot more from adolescence
> [sic] nowadays and provide them with a lot less
> social support . . . there still is an incredible need for
> emotional support. And by so many parents strug-
> gling to acquire the resources to provide them
> material support, they themselves have little room

left for their own emotional support and it also
reflects on the relationship that they have with their
adolescents.[22]

What a sad indictment of the adult generations! We need to make time for Millennials, particularly those who feel lonely and disconnected. We need to be willing to risk getting emotionally and relationally connected with them. In subsequent chapters, we will explore a helpful outline of mentoring styles and how adults can implement these styles in order to make a positive relational connection with the next generation.

CHAPTER FOUR

The Full Spectrum:
Living in the Postmodern Era

IF CHRISTIANS ARE TO MINISTER EFFECTIVELY IN THE SOCIETY AROUND THEM, they must understand the times. Even Scripture tells us the importance of "understanding the present time" (Romans 13:11). This is especially vital when considering the opportunity and challenge of preparing the Millennial generation for mature adulthood and increasing their potential to be the next hero generation.

Whether we're focusing on the positive end of the spectrum (the promise and potential of the Millennial generation) or the negative end (the "lost children" of the Millennial generation), it's obvious this generation is growing up in an era that is experiencing tremendous changes. Sadly, "most Christians do not perceive the Church to be in the midst of the most severe struggle it has faced in centuries," observes Christian researcher George Barna.[1]

A Societal Shift

A few years ago, I attended a conference for mission executives responsible for recruiting and screening the next generation of missionaries. The hot topic of conversation during the conference was the emerging challenges of working with these young recruits. It was obvious to many of these executives that significant changes were taking place in the recruits' perceptions and attitudes — not just the normal "generational differences," but ones that appeared symptomatic of deeper societal shifts.

Indeed, the new Gen X and Millennial generation of missionaries demonstrated two clear differences that necessitated a shift in thinking among mission leaders: first, their reluctance to make long-term commitments (defined as "lifetime" with past generations), and second, their insistence that they receive adequate "member care" to foster a sense of community and care for their emotional, physical, and spiritual needs while on the mission field. It seemed the era of the self-sufficient "pioneer missionary," who would come home only upon retirement or death, was no longer a reality.

The keynote speaker at the conference was a thirty-something pastor who dressed in faded blue jeans, sported several earrings, and had dyed hair that was spiked provocatively. The audience, on the other hand, consisted mostly of conservative, buttoned-down, fifty- and sixty-somethings dressed in suits and ties. Anyone walking into the auditorium at that moment would have wondered if communication could ever happen in such a circumstance, yet the audience hung on every word.

This man pastored what he called a "postmodern church" with a congregation almost exclusively comprising Gen Xers and Millennials. He shared some of the challenges that he was facing as a young pastor and how a sea change had taken place in the perspectives and attitudes of the younger generations as compared to the generation of their parents (the Boomer generation). He attributed much of this differing perspective to the Gen X and Millennial generations having spent their formative years growing up in a postmodern era.[2]

Just What Is Postmodernism?

A description of this postmodern era is best accomplished by contrasting the postmodern perception of truth to that of past eras. First, there was the *premodern era* (before A.D. 1700), best illustrated by a priest who understood right from wrong and spoke the truth authoritatively. Society at large would unequivocally accept the word of the moral leader; questioning the concept of absolute truth would have been unthinkable.

Next came the *modern era* (1700 to 1970), best illustrated by a scientist who used the scientific method to search for the truth. No longer would the word of a "priest," or a moral leader, be unequivocally accepted. Instead, it first had to be tested and validated. The concept of absolute truth was still accepted *as long as* it had been proven by the scientific method.

The third, and current, era is the *postmodern era* (1970 to present), best illustrated by a rock star trying to find truth in poetry, music, art, and most importantly, *within himself*. In this era, the concept of absolute truth is completely rejected because truth is whatever you feel is right for you. As such, there simply cannot be any form of transcendent, absolute truth that imposes its authority on everyone.

An eye-opening illustration of the postmodern mindset is a story related by Chuck Colson. Colson was having dinner with a media personality, and as he talked with him about Christianity he explained how he had come to Christ. "Obviously Jesus worked for you," Bill (not his real name) replied, but went on to tell Colson about someone he knew whose life had been turned around by New Age spirituality. "Crystals, channeling—it worked for her. Just like your Jesus."[3] Colson tried to explain the difference, but got nowhere. He broached the topic of death and eternal life, but Bill did not believe in heaven or hell and wasn't intimidated by the prospect of dying. Colson explained the concept of biblical truth, but Bill did not believe in the Bible or any other spiritual authority.

Finally, Colson mentioned the Woody Allen movie *Crimes and Misdemeanors,* about a killer who silences his conscience by concluding that life is nothing more than the survival of the fittest—and Bill became more thoughtful. Colson followed up with examples from Tolstoy and C. S. Lewis on the reality of moral law—and Bill showed more interest. Then Colson cited the epistle of Romans, on the human inability to keep the law—and Bill at last paid close attention to the teachings of Scripture. Although Bill did not become a Christian, Colson felt that he at least had broken through some of his defenses. The difficulty was in finding a common frame of reference. Certainly, the usual evangelistic approaches did not work. "My experience," said Colson, "is a sobering illustration of how resistant the modern mind has become to the Christian message."[4]

Indeed, times have changed. Our traditional evangelistic methods are not as effective as they once were. And it's especially important for us to remember this as we seek to pass on biblical values to Millennials and prepare them for the challenges ahead. Let's take a closer look at the postmodern way of thinking and how this can shape the heart and mind of a Millennnial.

How Does a Postmodern Think?

It is hard to share the truth with people who believe that truth is relative ("Jesus works for you; crystals work for her"). It's difficult to proclaim the forgiveness of sins to people who believe they have no sin to forgive ("morality is relative"). It's hard to convince people of the uniqueness of Jesus Christ when they believe in many roads to God. Indeed, by the early 1990s, 66 percent of Americans believed that "there is no such thing as absolute truth." Among young adults (between eighteen and twenty-five), the percentage was even higher: 72 percent.[5]

Obviously, it is not just some ethereal-thinking philosophers who hold this deeply problematic view of truth, but the average person on the street. It is not a fringe element, but two-thirds of the American people. Moreover, the poll went on to show that the majority (53 percent) of those who called themselves evangelical Christians—those who said they believed in the authority of the Bible and knew Christ as their Savior—believed "there is no such thing as absolute truth."[6]

These polls suggest that something new and frightening has happened to our attitudes. As Gene Veith Jr. states in his book *Postmodern Times: A Christian Guide to Contemporary Thought and Culture,*

> While people have always committed sins, they at
> least acknowledged these were sins. A century ago
> a person may have committed adultery flagrantly
> and in defiance of God and man, but he would
> have admitted that what he was doing was a sin.
> What we have today is not only immoral behavior,
> but a loss of moral criteria. This is true even in the
> church. We face not only a moral collapse but a
> collapse of meaning. There are no absolutes.[7]

While modernists would "disprove" Christianity via the scientific method or academic inquiry, postmodernists attack Christianity on different grounds. Their most common critique is that "Christians think they have the only truth." They do not so much deny the claims of Christianity as they outright reject them because those claims purport to be absolute truth. They consider Christianity intolerant (trying to force its beliefs on other people) and, therefore, completely out of bounds for anyone who strives to intelligently construct a personal worldview.

In the postmodernist mindset, morality is a matter of desire. In other words, "What I want and what I choose is not only true for me but right for me." That different people want and choose different things means that truth and morality are relative, but "I have a right" to my desires. Conversely, "no one has the right" to criticize my desires and my choices. Thus tolerance becomes the ultimate virtue. The post-modernist sins are "being judgmental," "being narrow-minded," "thinking that you have the only truth," and "trying to enforce your idea of truth or values on anyone else." The only wrong idea is to believe in truth; the only transgression is to believe in sin. Postmodernists, therefore, reject Christianity on the same grounds that they reject modernism, with its scientific rationalism. Ironically, both Christians and modernists believe in truth, whereas postmodernists do not.[8]

What Happened to Jim

The postmodern perspective has shaped the hearts and minds of the Millennial generation in ways that would shock us. I learned this lesson firsthand when one of my best and brightest students returned to our international high school in Ecuador after completing his degree at a well-known and respected Christian liberal arts college. A son of missionaries, this twenty-one-year-old turned down four lucrative job offers, purchased an airline ticket, and returned to his old high school community because he had a burning question in his heart. The first evening in town happened to be on a Sunday so, out of force of habit, he decided to attend the evening service at the local English-speaking church.

The pastor noticed that he was in the congregation, and so he asked Jim (not his real name) to open the service in prayer. Jim was caught between a rock and a hard place because, at this point in his life, he no longer embraced the faith of his missionary parents. Not knowing the proper action to take, Jim decided not to embarrass the pastor and stood up and prayed an eloquent prayer.

Early Monday morning, Jim was waiting for me to arrive at my office. We embraced and greeted each other—I had not seen him since his high school graduation four years earlier—but I could tell that something was bothering him. Jim didn't mince words. "I'm no longer a Christian," he blurted out. He paused and choked up a bit, but then continued. "My parents did a great job sharing the gospel with me and they lived out their faith authentically. I also learned the truth here at school and that's why I've returned." He felt as if he were an actor in a drama and that he was merely playing his "Christian" role for the audience. "If I had been raised in a Buddhist home, I would be a devout Buddhist. If I had been raised in a Hindu home, I would be a devout Hindu. If I had been raised in a Muslim home, I would be a devout Muslim. What right do I have to believe that there is only one way to God?" Jim then looked me in the eye and asked a question that nearly took my breath away: "Dr. Egeler, I want to know if you really believe what you've been preaching all these years, or are you just role playing like I've done for the past fourteen years?"

It was then that I realized the struggle that Jim and his Millennial generation face in accepting the biblical truth that Jesus taught in John 14:6: "I am the way and the truth and the life. No one comes to the Father except through me." This generation has been raised in a postmodern era in which the doctrine of the uniqueness of Jesus Christ is considered extremely intolerant and therefore completely out of bounds. How can one possibly believe that Jesus is the *only* way to the Father? Tolerance teaches that there are many ways to God— especially that *your* way is the one that works for you.

Same Question, Different Questioner

After pausing to collect myself, I told Jim the following story about how I had been asked a nearly identical question almost ten years earlier. A Ph.D. student in a major Midwestern university at the time, I was taking a doctoral level course in classical social theory in which eight graduate students (I was the only Christian) were studying the writings of classic theorists such as Émile Durkheim, Karl Marx, and Max Weber. The teachings of Jesus were mocked and scorned in the classroom on a regular basis, but—I'm ashamed to admit—I was intimidated and "hid my candle under a bushel" by keeping silent. I was a modern-day Simon Peter.

Midway through the semester, the professor suddenly had an epiphany and came into class one day with new criteria for our term paper: write a paper on our "worldview," as he termed it, defending our personal perspective on sociology. In other words, we were to describe our perspective on why people act the way they do in groups and society at large, referring back to the classic sociologists that we had discussed in class.

I went home that evening knowing the gig was up. I either had to lie and continue to play my undercover role, or I had to tell the truth about what I believed. I decided that night I had to step out and be intellectually honest. I spent hours and hours researching the paper, realizing that I could not simply use the Bible as my basis for truth; the professor would surely find one source unacceptable. Besides, the term paper was to be 75 percent of the semester grade, so I also wanted to turn in a quality product.

On the last day of the semester, the professor walked into the classroom, threw the stack of eight term papers on his desk, and said, "I couldn't grade these—they were much too personal." At that point, my habit of remaining silent went out the window. "What do you mean—these were to be 75 percent of our grade and, besides, you asked for our personal perspective."

He looked at me with a combination of curiosity, frustration, and maybe even a hint of anger, and answered, "They *were* well written, but I realized that they reflected deeply held core values and were too personal to assign a grade. Your semester grade will simply reflect what would have been 25 percent of the criteria that had been assigned in the course syllabus." He then paused, eyed me directly, and said, "And I want to see you in my office after class." At that point, my knees began to quiver. Was he going to reprimand me for challenging his decision?

His office was a stereotypical college professor's office with books lining all of the walls. A dim bulb hung down over his desk as he leaned back in his chair while puffing on his pipe. He motioned for me to sit down, and he sat looking at me without saying a word. It felt like an eternity before he spoke, and when he did he asked me the same question Jim asked ten years later: "I want to know if you really believe what you wrote in this paper or are you just playing a role?"

He told about how he was raised in a Catholic home and had what he called "an experience with a supreme being" when he was a teenager. "I've spent a good part of my professional life trying to explain that experience away," he admitted, but a chord was struck deep within his soul when he read my paper. Did I really believe what I had written, or were these just intellectual ideas?

He went on to share how he had raised a son who was on his third marriage and who had just been released from drug rehabilitation. As a father, he felt partially responsible because he had never been able to provide his son with a sound, moral foundation on which to make lifestyle decisions. He didn't believe in absolute truth and, therefore, his son was supposed to figure out his own set of moral guidelines. After watching his son struggle, he knew that he was a failure as a father.

I didn't quite know how to respond; certainly, I was not expecting this question or the follow-up disclosure. Finally gathering my thoughts, I began to talk about the concept of truth and whether there are transcendent moral values that should govern human behavior. I pointed out that moral judgments keep asserting themselves, no matter how often one attempts to evade them. The very claim that sociologists make that certain power structures are oppressive, repeated over and over in scholarship, implies a moral principle: that it is not good to oppress people. I had quoted C. S. Lewis, from his classic *Mere Christianity,* and had pointed out Lewis's observation, "Whenever you find a man who says he does not believe in a real Right and Wrong, you will find the same man going back on this a moment later. He may break his promise to you, but if you try breaking one to him, he will be complaining, 'It's not fair.'"[9] My professor chuckled; he realized the truth in the statement.

Two hours later, we got around to the presuppositions underlying the existence of absolute truth. My professor continued to deny vehemently the concept of absolute truth, but he had to admit that such an approach had not been successful in his role as a father. As I left his office, he took my hand and, with tears in his eyes, said, "Son, don't ever lose what you have. I only wish I could take the same leap of faith, but I'm afraid of committing intellectual suicide."

In reflecting back on this conversation, I've often thought a parallel may exist to Jesus' words in Luke 18:24-25 when he said, "How hard it is for the rich to enter the kingdom of God! Indeed, it is easier for a camel to go through the eye of a needle than for a rich man to enter the kingdom of God." I've wondered if it's not easier for a camel to go through the eye of a needle than for a *smart* person to enter the kingdom of God. For most smart folks, the gospel message seems just too simple (even a child can understand it). The idea of taking a leap of faith is just not fair to those who want everything figured out.

By the way, I am *not* denigrating the importance of the cultivation of the Christian mind or denying the need for a vigorous apologetic of the Christian faith. I fully support J. P. Moreland when he stated, "According to the Bible, developing a Christian mind is part of the very essence of discipleship unto the Lord Jesus."[10] My point here is that, by faith, even a child can enter the kingdom of heaven, and such a simple message—salvation as a gift from God through the person of Jesus Christ—is often a stumbling block to the wise (like my professor) and to the postmodern (like Jim).

Other Postmodern Pitfalls

One clear consequence of denying the existence and authority of absolute truth can be found in the prevalence of lying in our culture today. Chuck Colson points out that some scholars believe the problem of lying arose out of the gradual adoption of a utilitarian ethic that began eroding the traditional Christian ethic of the West in the middle to late nineteenth century. This ethic says the (good) end justifies the means. In other words, if a lie helps more than it harms, then we should feel free to employ one. Colson goes on to point out that in the late twentieth century, the rise of postmodernist teaching on college campuses—truth is not merely irrelevant; it doesn't exist at all—exacerbated this problem. Indeed, those who assert that truth exists, and that telling falsehoods is wrong, are increasingly under assault. "Fact fetishists" is how New York University professor Thomas Bender characterizes people who insist on accuracy.[11]

Colson concludes by challenging authentic Christians to "help our neighbors understand what's behind the current propensity for lying: a worldview that denies the existence of truth itself, which merely exacerbates our human fallenness. And then we must point them to the Author of truth, the one who said, 'I am the Way, the Truth, and the Life.'"[12] In the same way, we need to accept the responsibility for pointing out this destructive worldview to the Millennial generation.

Another insight into the dangers of the postmodern mindset is the lesson we can learn from the Roman Empire. The Roman Empire was a very pluralistic society, and although they had lost their ancient virtues, Romans were extremely tolerant. The only people they could *not* tolerate were Christians. During the persecutions, Christians who refused to recant their faith had their legal rights suspended and could be instantly put to death under a legal system which was otherwise scrupulously fair.[13]

In his study of anti-Christian propaganda in imperial Rome, historian Stephen Benko maintains that one of the main reasons the early Christians were persecuted so vigorously was that they claimed to possess exclusive truth. In its decay, Roman culture had become something like our postmodern society, advocating cultural relativism (under Roman control, of course) and the validity of all religions (as long as everyone burned incense to Caesar). The Christians' refusal to accept the emperor's deity was bad enough. But what really angered the ancient Romans was the fact that these arrogant slaves actually claimed to possess the *only* truth.[14]

The early church, however, never compromised its message, despite its unpopularity. Thousands of Christians lost their lives, and evangelism efforts were understandably complicated by the fact that new converts could potentially face the death penalty. Nevertheless, people kept coming to Christ until the whole Roman Empire bowed before the lordship of Jesus Christ.[15] Could Christian young people of the Millennial generation be the same change-agents for the American postmodern culture as the early church was for the Roman Empire?

Postmodernism Run Amok

The strange saga of John Walker Lindh, the American Taliban warrior, is one that should give us pause, as it is a perfect illustration of where the foolishness of postmodern thinking can lead a Millennial. This is the story of a young man who forsook the comfortable life of Marin

County, California, for the wilds of Yemen and Afghanistan to fight with the Taliban against American and Afghani troops. One wonders how he could turn his back on his nation, his family, and his home.

The country came to discover that Lindh was from a family so steeped in postmodernist thinking that, as editorial columnist Mona Charon states, "they declined to impose their values even on themselves."[16] Like most Millennials, Lindh was deeply idealistic and wanted to commit to a cause; he wanted to be on the side of right. But in his experience and reading, his country was rarely in the right. In fact, the United States was the oppressor, the enslaver, and the imperialist. The Taliban was the team to belong to.

Clearly, the Lindh family is an extreme case, but as a postmodern family, what transcendent truth could they appeal to when their son made his own choice and cobbled together his own set of moral values? In fact, eager to provide their son with choices and to be supportive, the Lindhs enrolled John in an alternative high school. The school held no classes and required only that students meet once or twice a week with a tutor to discuss their independent research. John studied world cultures, and he soon developed an appreciation for and then a strong allegiance to Islam.[17]

With their emphasis on facilitating the development of an "open mind" and their adherence to the ultimate virtue of tolerance, the Lindhs would not (and could not) put their foot down when their sixteen-year-old dropped out of school, converted to Islam, and announced a desire to live in Yemen. As Charon so clearly articulates,

> On what grounds could the Lindhs have objected?
> Could they have argued that Christianity had a
> superior spiritual message? That would be ethno-

centrism. Could they object that Arab nations are notoriously anti-American? They weren't wild about America themselves. Could they maintain that parents have authority over minor children because they are parents? Not the Lindhs. Their highest value was "choice."[18]

John Walker Lindh clearly went further than his parents would have desired. The Lindhs were quite dismayed that he fought with the Taliban and trained with al-Qaeda. However, they should not have been surprised, because he simply went too far in the direction they had pointed him. As postmodernists, the Lindhs could not and did not provide the intellectual and spiritual commitment to absolute truth that would have given their son guidance during the vulnerable times in his life.

Meanwhile, Back at the Mission Conference

After the young postmodern pastor shared at the conference for mission executives, I went to him during a break and asked what he would advise for those parents and concerned adults raising a generation of Millennial kids. (As it turns out, he's a young father raising two Millennials of his own.) The key question in my mind was, "If this Millennial generation is so resistant to absolute truth, how do we go about teaching them biblical truth?"

"We need to unapologetically teach the truth," he said, "but we need to remember that it's even more important to *live* the truth." He used the analogy of twin pistons propelling a locomotive down the track. The adult generations need to preach the truth, live the truth, preach the truth, live the truth, preach the truth, live the truth.[19]

This next generation will not hear the truth anywhere else in our postmodern society than in our homes, in our churches, in our Christian schools, and in mentoring relationships. As such, the truth *has* to be proclaimed. However, if the truth is not lived, then we run the danger of this generation perceiving that it's just hypocrisy. And if they perceive the message as hypocritical, then woe to the adult generations, for we may be inoculating the next generation with small doses of Christianity only to keep them from catching the real thing.

As my young friend Jim so openly expressed, this next generation wants to see authenticity in adult lives and not just words. In sum, this is the essence of mentoring.

PART TWO

EMPOWERING

MILLENNIALS

CHAPTER FIVE

Understanding Mentoring

A COMMON MISPERCEPTION REGARDING THE PROCESS OF LEARNING IS THAT the job of "preaching the truth" is complete when truth has been communicated to the student or protégé. True learning, however, is not complete until the truth being taught has been *understood, fully appreciated, and internalized.* In other words, simply preaching the truth does not mean true learning has taken place.

For true learning to take root, the twelve inches between the head and the heart must be bridged. In order to produce real, authentic life change, it is not enough for the Millennial generation to just know; they must (1) believe what they know, (2) value what they believe, (3) internalize what they believe, and (4) appropriately act upon what they believe. This is especially relevant to the teaching of spiritual truths.

An Analogy from the World of Dental Hygiene

Teaching a child to brush his or her teeth is a simple illustration of this principle. As a father, I wanted my six-year-old son to develop the habit of brushing his teeth on a daily basis. Matthew had a difficult time remembering this nightly assignment, and Dad ended up constantly reminding him to complete the chore. Matthew knew (he had the head knowledge) that brushing his teeth was important, but he didn't really believe it. Knowing this was the case, I decided to include Matthew in a trip to the dentist for my older son, Andrew.

Matthew was pretty excited about this excursion, anxious to experience every sensation in the dentist's office. He could hardly sit still. Finally, the dental assistant came into the waiting room and led us to the room where Andrew was seated in the dentist chair. Matthew alertly watched the dentist open his brother's mouth to begin his inspection.

Soon the dentist announced, "Well, it looks like we've got two cavities here, Andrew." Matthew paid rapt attention when the dentist pulled out a syringe and injected some medicine into Andrew's mouth to numb it. His eyes widened further and his little body began to tense when the dentist hooked up the drill, opened Andrew's mouth, and began to work on the first cavity. As the dentist was finishing the process of filling the last cavity, he asked, "Andrew, have you been brushing your teeth every night?" (Of course Andrew couldn't respond; his mouth was full of dental instruments.) "You know, if you don't brush your teeth regularly, you'll have more cavities that I'll need to fill during your next visit."

It was at that point Matthew began to *believe* that brushing his teeth was important. Over the next several months, he diligently brushed his teeth every night without a single reminder from Dad.

Six months later, however, Matthew's memory of watching his brother have his cavities filled began to fade, and the importance of regular tooth brushing diminished. Now it was Matthew's turn to see the dentist. He was quite apprehensive, fearing he would suffer his brother's fate, but when the dentist finished his inspection he remarked, "Matthew, you don't have any cavities to fill and I'm sure it's because you've been brushing your teeth. Way to go!"

After this verbal and experiential affirmation, Matthew not only began to believe that regularly brushing his teeth was important, but he also began to *value* and *internalize* the importance of the habit. Because he valued and internalized it, Matthew now began to independently *act upon* the belief. In other words, he faithfully brushed his teeth every night.

What made the difference for my son? It was his experience of seeing the personal relevance of the truth he was being taught. That same principle applies when teaching spiritual truths to the next generation. Truth will not be believed, valued, and internalized until the young person sees its personal relevance. This is where the process of mentoring is so critical. Effective mentors should be authentic examples of living the truth and then provide their protégés with the opportunity to live it as well. The older generation needs to simultaneously employ the "twin pistons" of living the truth and preaching the truth—the essence of mentoring.

Breaching the Wall

"You choose your beliefs, your neatly tied package of what can and cannot be. With these beliefs we weave the fabric of our religion. But what if God refuses to be defined by what we consider believable? What if truth is not something we create, but something we discover and embrace?"[1] Thus began a full-page ad in *The Gazette*, my hometown newspaper. The first two statements crystallize the concept of truth for many Millennials. The two provocative questions that concluded the advertisement, however, should shake any Millennial to the core if he or she is willing to honestly reflect on them.

But how do we get the Millennial generation to that place of honest reflection? Leith Anderson, a megachurch pastor and church growth consultant, proposes that the contemporary generation best understands the truth when it is illustrated by stories that include practical applications. He suggests that because this generation tends not to think in a systematic way or pay close attention to rational argumentation, we can best approach ideas issue by issue and through the influence of our relationships. Role models, mentors, and friends shape people's thinking—for better or worse—more than objective thinking does.[2]

Gene Veith Jr., author of *Postmodern Times: A Christian Guide to Contemporary Thought and Culture,* supports the importance of relationships in breaching the wall of rejection that postmodernists have raised against Christianity:

> The young man who says he believes the Bible but who also believes in reincarnation might come back to orthodoxy through a Bible study focusing on the specific issue of life after death. As he reads the Word of God, the Holy Spirit will be at work. In the meantime, by forming close relationships with a pastor whom he respects and solid Christians whom he loves, the young man will likely come under the influence of their orthodoxy.[3]

Josh McDowell stresses the importance of making a "relational connection" when instructing the Millennial generation.[4] Jesus Christ pointed out the importance of loving relationships as a mark of discipleship when he said, "By this all men will know that you are my disciples, if you love one another" (John 13:35). The siren song of tolerance that this generation has heard in our postmodern age makes presenting absolute truth very difficult. However, these young people crave connection and authenticity, and will respond to a genuine demonstration of the love Jesus emphasized.

So exactly what do we mean when we use the term "mentoring"? Paul Stanley and Robert Clinton, authors of *Connecting: The Mentoring Relationships You Need to Succeed in Life*, propose an expanded definition of the word. For them, mentoring is "a relational process in which a mentor, who knows or has experienced something, transfers that something (resources of wisdom, information, experience, confidence, insight, relationships, status, etc.) to a mentoree, at an appropriate time and manner, so that it facilitates development or empowerment."[5] Let's explore three key phrases of Stanley and Clinton's definition in greater depth: "a relational process," "at an appropriate time and manner," and "so that it facilitates development or empowerment."

A Relational Process

The first key phrase in the definition is "a relational process." This relational process, or connection, is the foundation upon which a mentoring relationship is built. Some common variables important to a relational connection include time, proximity, needs, shared values, and mutual goals. Underlying these variables, however, are three dynamics that are vital to establishing and maintaining a healthy mentoring relationship: (1) mutual attraction, (2) protégé's responsiveness, and (3) mutual accountability.[6]

A mutual attraction is the necessary starting point in any relationship. The protégé is often attracted to the mentor for his or her experience and skills, perceived wisdom, and modeling of values, character, and integrity. In turn, a mentor is often attracted to the teachable spirit and potential in a protégé. Without a protégé's willingness and teachable heart, there is little a mentor can accomplish.

A mentor must realize that a mutual attraction and teachable heart are not his or her responsibility. A mentor can work to foster a mutual attraction but the protégé must respond in kind. Likewise, a mentor can teach and model the importance of a teachable heart but it's incumbent upon the protégé to implement this principle into his or her own life. This is simply something that the mentor cannot do for the protégé.

Schools, churches, or other institutions sometimes implement mentoring programs by assigning each protégé to a mentor so that no one falls through the cracks. Invariably, these programs struggle for two key reasons: it's impossible to *prescribe* a mutual attraction and to *impose* a teachable spirit. These two variables must be present, and they cannot be programmed or taught after the fact.

The irony and tragedy is that many of the Millennials who could most benefit from mentoring are just not ready for such a relationship—they don't yet have a teachable heart and, therefore, resist any mutual attraction with an adult. In the meantime, adults ought to continue to offer the possibility of a friendship, but only when a mutual attraction and a teachable spirit finally fall into place can the process of mentoring begin. Again, it's important to remember that, beneath the surface, every young person yearns for adult relationships; often it just takes time before an angry and rebellious teenager will put this desire into action.

The final component in ensuring a vibrant relational connection is accountability. At the outset of the mentoring relationship, mentor and protégé should honestly communicate expectations and schedule periodic reviews. Such a structure avoids possible misunderstandings as well as facilitates the protégé's progress and the eventual closure of the mentoring process. The importance of accountability increases in significance depending on the particular mentoring style being used (more on this later). In simplest terms, the more intentional and the greater the time commitment made to the relationship, the greater the need for accountability.

Adults sometimes find it threatening to try to establish a relational connection with the next generation. Dr. Donald Lichi, president of Chapel Hill Christian School, presents four simple and practical suggestions for establishing a friendship:

First, learn to make teenagers feel important. Be genuinely interested in them and their lives. This alone is a huge step.

Second, express your positive feelings about the young person. Notice special things about the person, recognize her talents and skills, look for positive qualities. Then, look for opportunities to share these qualities with the young person and others. This positive conversation is an investment in a relational connection.

Third, spend time with the young person. Invite him to do something that he enjoys, or just do a special favor for him. Of course, you'll need to make the effort to get to know him in order to find out what he enjoys.

Fourth, don't be afraid to share this friendship with others. If you're not possessive, you'll include others in the mentoring process as well as strengthening a healthy bond between you and your young friend.[7]

Dr. Lichi also teaches about the cycle of friendship that occurs as a relationship matures. If a mutual attraction is beginning, the first step in a cycle of friendship is to build rapport. The next step entails getting to know each other—the point when the adult can begin to become intentional and implement the practical suggestions outlined earlier. The final stages involve mutual dependence and meeting mutual needs.

In truth, a deep and healthy adult-to-Millennial relationship benefits the adult as much as the young person. When adults take the risk and become involved in "downward" mentoring (reaching down to the next generation), their own thinking is challenged by fresh ideas and their own lives are enhanced.

Just Chill

Upon returning to the United States after years of teaching overseas, I learned firsthand how downward mentoring relationships can challenge an adult's thinking. To help my son's adjustment to a new school, I had volunteered to coach his sixth-grade soccer team. I left work a bit early on the first day of practice and broke into a cold sweat as I pulled into the school parking lot, realizing that other than my son I didn't know a single kid on the team.

I parked the car and walked over to the horde of students leaving school, and finally noticed a small clump of boys standing together with their backpacks and band instruments in a pile in front of them. (Because the school did not own athletic fields, the coach was expected to load into his vehicle all the students' paraphernalia, and then have the kids jog as a group to a public park close to the school.) As I walked toward the boys, one of them shouted out, "Are you our soccer coach?" I answered back, "I sure am!" With that, the boys circled around and proceeded to greet me with a loud "Whazuuuup?"

Though I was familiar with the popular television commercial of the time, their greeting made me a bit apprehensive. I was used to an academic setting where I had been treated with a measure of respect. No one would have dared greet me with "Whazuuuup?"—most definitely not a bunch of squirmy sixth-graders. Was this a lack of respect?

Once I reached the park, I unloaded all the gear and waited for the boys to arrive. As they bent down, catching their breath, I gruffly asked all of them to stand up and look me in the eye. By my tone of voice, they knew I meant business. A hush fell over the group; I had their undivided attention. Imagine their surprise when the next word out of my mouth was an enthusiastic "Whazuuuup?" Immediately, they realized I had a sense of humor, and they all laughed hysterically. That brief interaction set the tone for establishing a relational connection with these young men for the duration of the season. And it reminded me that I needed to chill out and enjoy my time with them.

At the Core of Downward Mentoring

A downward mentoring relationship tests an adult's flexibility, especially when it comes to considering new solutions to familiar problems. Are you willing to have your thinking challenged? Can you remain open to fresh ideas? A downward mentoring relationship encourages a special kind of accountability. As you consciously serve as a role model to young people, are you able to maintain your consistency and integrity? Finally, because the Millennial generation places great emphasis on commitment to a cause, a downward mentoring relationship can stretch adults who involve themselves with these young men and women.[8] Are you willing to lay cynicism aside and have your ideals inspired? Bottom line, a healthy downward mentoring relationship should be energy producing rather than energy draining.

Joe's Story

I first began to understand the depth of a Millennial's yearning for adult connection and how invigorating a downward mentoring relationship could be when I met Joe (not his real name). An orphan adopted by his missionary parents as an infant, Joe was a very intelligent young man who grew up speaking five languages. But during high school, he began to run with the wrong crowd. As his principal, I sensed that he was involved in all sorts of activity contrary to the school's code of conduct (though he was always smart enough to seldom get caught). I was also the varsity soccer coach, and during Joe's senior year I was surprised to see his name scrawled on the list of hopefuls trying out for the team. We had a very competitive soccer program, so I knew it was going to be a real long shot for Joe to make the team.

The three days of tryouts included a fitness evaluation at the end of each practice. Joe was not in shape, and because his personal habits were not conducive to physical fitness, these evaluations were taxing for him. During a particularly grueling session on the final day, Joe just could not keep up. Midway through a series of sprints, he abruptly left his group and suffered the humiliation of "losing his lunch" in front of all his peers. But rather than just pack it in and quit, Joe valiantly rejoined his group. It was obvious to everyone that for some reason Joe desperately wanted to be a part of the team.

Occasionally, I would save a spot on the roster for a "project" kid, and at that moment I decided Joe would be my project kid that year. The irony was that the person responsible for discipline in the high school (me!) was going to coach the kid most involved in breaking the rules.

As the season progressed, Joe at last got into shape and, demonstrating some latent athletic ability, started to contribute to the team's success. The season finale was a soccer tournament hosted in a jungle city that was a six-hour ride away through the Andes Mountains. As we were loading up, I noticed that Joe knifed ahead of everyone else to claim the front passenger seat in the van I was driving. Surprisingly, he was a chatterbox the whole way. At every refueling stop, he would jump out of the van, wash the windshield, put gas in the vehicle, and ask if he could be otherwise helpful.

When we arrived at our destination, Joe asked, "Coach, have you already finalized all the sleeping arrangements?"

"Not really," I replied. "Is there another teammate that you would like to request as a roommate?"

Joe lowered his gaze and nervously scuffed the ground. "Is there anyone bunking with you?"

I was a bit surprised. "Why, do you want to room with me?"

In almost a whisper, he replied, "Yeah."

I could see that Joe was aching to spend some time with me, so roommates we became.

On the way home from the tournament, all the boys in our van but Joe had drifted off to sleep. "Coach, I'm going to try to stay awake so that I can keep you company," he said.

"Thanks, Joe," I said. "These mountain roads can be pretty treacherous, and I would appreciate some company." Because we had established a rapport through the week, after having spent a significant amount of time together, I sensed an opportunity to speak to Joe's heart. "Joe, you and I both know you've been involved in activity that I would not consider appropriate."

Joe smiled a wry smile and replied, "You're right. I guess I'm just too slick to get caught."

I nodded my head in agreement, and then asked, "Joe, can you tell me why you're involved in this type of activity?"

Joe paused, drew in his breath, and responded, "I don't know, Coach. It's just that I got sucked in with a group of friends outside of school who are really loyal to me—but I know that they haven't been the best influence."

"Then why do you hang out with these guys?"

Joe was silent for a long time, and his voice cracked with emotion when he answered. "I just don't fit in at school, and I know that my friends outside of school really care about me. I feel that no one at school really knows who I am or really cares about me. In fact, I wonder sometimes if my dad even cares about me. It just seems that he doesn't have time for me." His shoulders began to shake. I thought he was through speaking but he continued, barely choking out the words. "I really think my dad loves his computer more than me since he spends more time with that machine than he does with me."

I reached over and put my hand on his shoulder and said, "Joe, I can't answer that for you, but I want you to know that I really care about you." Joe nodded his head, and we continued to travel in silence. Despite the lack of verbal communication the rest of the trip, I knew we had made a significant relational connection.

Joe went on to graduate, and a number of teachers breathed a sigh of relief when he received his diploma. He had been a thorn in the flesh for most of the staff during the bulk of his high school career.

Just before the next Christmas vacation, a gentleman burst into my office with a beaming smile on his face. It was Joe's father. "Joe called last night," he said, "and he asked that I let you know that he's going to stop by and see you when he comes home."

"Can you tell me why he wants to see me?" I asked.

His father hesitated a moment before saying, "No, Joe said that he wants to tell you the news personally."

A week later, Joe visited me at school. I hardly recognized him because his demeanor and countenance had changed so drastically. He was a different person inside and out.

When we sat down in my office, Joe told me an amazing story of how he had an encounter with God that dramatically changed his life. In the middle of the night, he had awakened in a sweat, sensing that God was speaking to him. He knew that *now* was the time to completely surrender himself to the lordship of Christ. So, with sweat pouring down his face, he knelt down beside his bed and gave his life to Jesus. It was an experience that seemed a bit like a modern-day version of Saul's experience on the Damascus road.

Joe never looked back. He went on to enroll in a Christian college and graduated four years later. Several years after his graduation, I had dinner with Joe and he introduced me to his fiancée, a beautiful

Christian girl. That evening I followed up on our long-ago conversation on the mountain road. "Remember when everyone had fallen asleep on the way back and I asked why you were behaving the way you were? Do you recall your answer?"

Joe nodded, and as he looked at his fiancée, he said, "Coach, I told you that no one really cared about me and that I thought my dad loved his computer more than me. But I want you to hear the real story. My dad never failed to tuck me in at night and to pray with me. There were times that I came home in the wee hours of the morning, completely stoned or drunk, and he would be waiting up for me. Rather than giving me the third degree or kicking me out of the house, he would help me get into bed and then kneel down beside my bed and pray for me." His voice now thick with emotion, he said, "I used to hate it when he did that. I didn't want anything to do with God. But Dad's prayers continued to haunt me. Despite my protests to the contrary, I knew deep down inside that my dad loved me. I was just running away from God and I took it out on my father. I'm so thankful now that he never gave up on me. Outwardly, I despised him for it, but deep inside, the love that he demonstrated was something I desperately needed."

I'll never forget what Joe shared with me that evening. I'll always remember the patient love of a father for his son who outwardly despised and rejected him—much like the prodigal son. I'll also remember that, even though it appeared that this Millennial had a hardened heart, deep down inside he craved acceptance, love, and respect from the significant adults in his life. The lesson for me was that I needed to continue to risk establishing relational connections with Millennials, and then to be ready for that moment when they are ready to respond with mutual attraction and a responsive heart.

Stanley and Clinton, Continued

After "relational connection," Stanley and Clinton continue their expanded definition of mentoring with two additional key phrases: "at an appropriate time and manner" and "so that it facilitates development or empowerment." The first of these phrases carries with it the idea of differing levels of involvement and greater degrees of intensity that I mentioned earlier. Stanley and Clinton outline a helpful model of mentoring styles that follows a progression of increasing intentionality (in terms of goals and objectives) and increasing intensity (particularly in terms of time commitment)—with the ultimate goal of empowering the protégé:

LEVEL ONE: Passive Mentoring
- Contemporary Style
- Historical Style

LEVEL TWO: Occasional Mentoring
- Counseling Style
- Teaching Style
- Sponsoring Style

LEVEL THREE: Intensive Mentoring
- Discipling Style
- Spiritual Guiding Style
- Coaching Style

The first level of mentoring is called "passive mentoring" (explored further in chapter 6). There are two distinct styles of passive mentoring: the contemporary model and the historical model.[9] The contemporary model is someone living who mentors, without a deliberate effort, simply by living a life that provides a model for a protégé. In the historical model the mentor is no longer living, yet mentors a protégé through his or her legacy. These mentoring styles can be thought of as "hero" styles because the protégé looks to the mentor from afar, and there is little or no *mutual* intentionality or intensity in the relationship. In fact, these are the only mentoring styles not predicated on a relational connection. Every other mentoring style requires that there be a significant relational connection for the process to be effective.

Of course, attraction is just as necessary in the passive model of mentoring. What sets the passive model apart is that the attraction is one-way—the protégé is attracted to the mentor and not vice versa. What attracts the protégé under the contemporary model is that the mentor's Christlike approach to his or her personal life, ministry, or profession not only serves as an example but also inspires emulation. The attraction under the historical model is a past life that teaches dynamic principles and values for life, ministry, and profession.

The contemporary model of mentoring is one that every authentic Christian should embrace. It is really *lifestyle* mentoring. As already emphasized, this is especially important when relating to Millennials who are sensitive to any form of hypocrisy and are yearning to make an all-out commitment to something that is authentic.

The second level of mentoring is called "occasional mentoring" (explored further in chapter 7), in which the intentionality and intensity of the relationship between protégé and mentor is more significant than in the passive level of mentoring. There are three distinct styles of occasional mentoring: counseling, teaching, and sponsoring.

In the counseling style, the mentor strives to empower the protégé through timely advice and correct perspectives on oneself, others, circumstances, and ministry. In the teaching style, the mentor strives to empower the protégé through the knowledge and understanding of a particular subject. In the sponsoring style, the mentor strives to empower the protégé through career guidance and protection, as the protégé becomes a leader within an organization.

The third and final level of mentoring is called "intensive mentoring" (explored further in chapter 8), in which the intentionality and intensity of the relationship between protégé and mentor is more significant than in any other style. There are three types of intensive mentoring: discipling, spiritual guiding, and coaching.

In the discipling style, the mentor strives to empower the protégé through understanding the basics of following Christ. In the spiritual guiding style, the mentor strives to empower the protégé through accountability, direction, and insight for questions, commitments, and decisions affecting spirituality and maturity. Finally, in the coaching style, the mentor provides motivation and imparts skills and application to meet a specific task or challenge.

Dispensing Grace

In his book *What's So Amazing About Grace?*, Philip Yancey develops a word picture that provides the adult generations with a powerful reminder for mentoring the Millennial generation.

> A phrase used by both Peter and Paul has become
> one of my favorite images from the New Testament.
> We are to administer, or "dispense," God's grace, say
> the two apostles. The image brings to mind one of

the old-fashioned "atomizers" women used before the perfection of spray technology. Squeeze a rubber bulb, and droplets of perfume come shooting out of the fine holes at the other end. A few drops suffice for a whole body; a few pumps change the atmosphere in a room. That is how grace should work, I think. It does not convert the entire world or an entire society, but it does enrich the atmosphere. Now I worry that the prevailing image of Christians has changed from that of a perfume atomizer to a different spray apparatus: the kind used by insect exterminators. *There's a roach!* Pump, spray, pump, spray. *There's a spot of evil!* Pump, spray, pump, spray. Some Christians I know have taken on the task of "moral exterminator" for the evil-infested society around them.[10]

Our challenge is to uncompromisingly teach absolute truth while coming across not as bug spray but as the perfume of Christ. Yet how would the average Millennial characterize the adult generations? If we walked into a room, would a Millennial sense grace (the perfume of Christ) in our lifestyle? Or would he or she sense condemnation (bug spray)? If the Millennial generation begins to view our "preaching the truth" as a form of bug spray, then as mentioned in an earlier chapter, we're inoculating them with small doses of Christianity while unknowingly keeping them from catching the real thing.

We would do well to heed the apostles' exhortation to dispense God's grace as we teach absolute truth to the Millennial generation — so they "catch the real thing."

CHAPTER SIX

Passive Mentoring

LEVEL ONE: Passive Mentoring
- Contemporary Style
- Historical Style

LEVEL TWO: Occasional Mentoring
- Counseling Style
- Teaching Style
- Sponsoring Style

LEVEL THREE: Intensive Mentoring
- Discipling Style
- Spiritual Guiding Style
- Coaching Style

DR. VERNARD GANT, DIRECTOR OF URBAN SCHOOL SERVICES FOR THE Association of Christian Schools International, is an excellent example of the important role passive mentoring can play in a person's life. Gant says he is in Christian education today "by way of conclusion and not by default."[1] It was a long road coming to this conclusion, however, as Gant experienced a mentoring void that began during his formative years in the projects of Mobile, Alabama, continued through his undergraduate studies in Bible college and seminary training, and was perpetuated during his ministry years. He felt that, in large part, his formal education had provided him with good information but precious little preparation in life experience and practical training—particularly from an African-American perspective.

Gant came to know Jesus Christ as his personal Savior as a teenager. His father had become a recruiter for the Coast Guard and would annually have a booth at the Alabama State Fair. During the summer after Gant's junior year of high school, an evangelistic ministry had a booth across from his father's. On the last day of the fair, one of the ladies came over and shared the gospel message with Gant, and he accepted the gift of salvation.

Gant was passionate about living a genuine Christian life and sensed that God wanted him involved in full-time Christian ministry. The only college in Gant's frame of reference that provided this type of training was located in South Carolina, and after he enrolled, it was quite evident that he was the only African-American male on campus. Gant went on to complete his seminary training, and during his early years of ministry, he realized that he still did not have many personal mentors—particularly African-American males who could serve as ministry models.

From Nehemiah to Boston U.

It was at this point in his life that Gant developed the strategy of looking to historical and contemporary models as his mentors. He eventually termed these models "distant mentors" because he had no one nearby to call on for wisdom, insight, or direction. Dr. Martin Luther

King Jr. and Nehemiah became Gant's historical mentors. Dr. Glenn Loury, professor of economics at Boston University, became his contemporary passive mentor. (Dr. Loury was still alive, but Gant did not know him personally.)

Gant did not start with this strategy consciously in mind. Instead, it grew naturally from his love for reading, studying, and research analysis. The speeches and writings of these three men struck a chord deep in his soul. Upon coming across an initial piece of work by one of them, for weeks at a time Gant would regularly read or listen to anything he could get his hands on by that author or speaker.

During these periods of intense reading and inquiry, Gant implemented skills he learned in his seminary hermeneutics class. These skills, which anyone can use when seeking to learn from historical or contemporary mentors, were what Gant called the 2 P, 3 R, and Q/A ("pray," "preview," "read," "reread," "review," and "question and answer").

When beginning the process of reading a written piece or listening to a sermon or speech by one of his passive mentors, Gant first prayed and asked for the illumination of the Holy Spirit. Second, he quickly previewed the material to develop a feel for the overall theme and context. Third, Gant thoroughly read, or listened to, the piece of writing or speech from beginning to end. The fourth step entailed rereading, or again listening to, the piece while making mental notes or taking written notes. Fifth, he reviewed the material through the lens of the mental or written notes. And finally, he returned to the piece with specific questions in mind (drafted from the notes developed in previous steps) and sought answers to those questions. Out of this "question and answer" session, Gant developed a list of "top-ten" principles from each of his passive mentors. During times of quiet reflection, he would imagine sitting down across from each mentor and having a conversation with him as together they reviewed these principles.

As a historical mentor, Nehemiah modeled leadership and vision for Gant—particularly as Gant considered the parallels between Nehemiah's "city in ruins" and the current decay in America's urban centers. As in Nehemiah's time, the people of God have the resources and abilities to make a difference but they need leadership and vision.

Gant's other historical mentor, Dr. King, taught him never to lose hope in the struggle for social justice. Dr. King helped Gant to keep his focus pure and to remember why he was placed in his role as a leading Christian educator—to address the plight of the urban poor. Dr. King also taught him how to channel his feelings of isolation and loneliness into times of reflection and meditation. For Gant, these desert experiences serve as times of "redemptive suffering" when he is taught the deeper lessons of the soul.

Gant's contemporary mentor, Dr. Glenn Loury, presented a prescription for the progress of African-Americans in which he emphasized the importance of intellectual and social capital, or potential, that must be maximized to allow individuals to flourish. This capital can only realize its full potential through the empowerment of the poor through a process of self-help.

Gant took Dr. Loury's paradigm one step further by asserting that the potential and promise of the next generation of urban kids can only be truly maximized through a Christ-centered education. If Christ-centered education is a viable option for urban children, who have little hope and limited opportunities, then these children can be empowered to maximize their intellectual and social capital. Christian education, therefore, is the key to providing self-help for those who deserve a chance in America's decaying urban centers.

Subliminal Modeling

In some cases, the protégé is not even aware of the contemporary mentor's influence on his or her life. In their book *Connecting: The Mentoring Relationships You Need to Succeed in Life*, Paul Stanley and Robert Clinton call this "subliminal modeling."[2] In such an instance, the mentor can influence a protégé simply by association or working together.

This was powerfully illustrated to me recently when I shared a meal with a former student, Kevin, who had graduated from college and was preparing to go back overseas as a missionary. As Kevin was reflecting on his high school years, I found out that I had been one of his contemporary mentors by demonstrating crisis leadership during one of the darkest periods of our lives. Because I had not been intentional about mentoring Kevin, I had never even realized he was watching me.

During Kevin's final year of high school, his class spent a week at the beach together. This was not merely "fun in the sun," but a time the school set aside each year so the senior class might have an opportunity for closure and good-byes. Nearly all of the students enrolled in the school were Third Culture Kids (TCKs), who grew up in a culture other than their parents' passport culture. Though TCKs share many common benefits, including an expanded worldview, proficient cross-cultural skills, and the ability to speak several languages, they also generally endure a lifetime of good-byes at a young age. As a result, our international school implemented a curriculum that taught kids about the transition process, the natural feelings of grief that one encounters, and how to address those feelings from a healthy perspective.

I was invited to go on this particular trip as one of the adult sponsors. As in past years, the seniors wanted to spend their evenings walking and talking on the beach while the sun slipped over the horizon.

We ensured that the students took security precautions and that they went out in groups of no fewer than six that included males and at least one adult. Little did we know, but two criminals had been stalking our kids the entire week. On the last evening, they came out of the darkness and, armed with weapons, assaulted two of our students.

I'll never forget the haunting cry for help as one of the eyewitnesses came to find me. "Mr. Egeler. Mr. Egeler. Come quick! Something bad has happened!" Out of concern for everyone's safety, I mandated that all of the students and sponsors gather together in the chapel on the compound. As Kevin and his classmates were filing in to the small meeting room, I wondered what I would say to more than fifty teenagers who had just seen the implications of raw evil. I simply shared that we serve a loving God who sometimes allows bad things to happen to good people and that we needed to go to him in prayer for healing and comfort.

As groups of students knelt and began to pray, I sensed the Holy Spirit descending on the room—just like in the book of Acts. I haven't been in a prayer meeting like that before or since. It was a clear demonstration of God's comfort; when the night is the darkest, his light shines the brightest. And that was only the beginning of God's grace, as we watched him minister to the students who had been accosted, their parents back home, and the teacher who had been held at gunpoint during the attack.

When Bad Things Happen—
The Lesson Continues

Our next challenge was proceeding with the many graduation activities. In consultation with all involved, we decided that we were not going to let evil ruin this special event in the lives of Kevin and his classmates. Phil was our salutatorian that year and we had met several times earlier in the semester to review potential topics for his address. He was pretty nervous anyway, and his fears were not allayed a bit when I asked him to consider sharing some of his very difficult early life experiences with his classmates and the school community. Nevertheless, he decided to take the risk of being vulnerable and entitled his address, "Becoming Bitter or Better—When Bad Things Happen to Good People."

However, Phil began to wonder if he should be so open about his negative experiences when the pain of this recent tragedy was still so fresh. I recommended that he speak with the students involved in the incident and get their permission to share from his heart. They willingly granted his request.

At the commencement ceremony, Phil stood to speak amid the typical rustling of programs. Once he had begun, a hush fell over the audience. As he neared his conclusion, you could hear a pin drop in the auditorium. Phil shared how, as a young child, he had pulled a large pot of boiling liquid down on top of himself and suffered severe burns over most of his body. The doctors did not expect him to live, but God mercifully spared his life.

Having to undergo a series of painful skin grafts through most of his elementary school years, Phil became inwardly angry and developed a spirit of bitterness—particularly against God. Why would God allow such a tragedy to happen to an innocent young boy? Hadn't his parents made the sacrifice to become missionaries to serve God? Why would he allow their little boy to suffer in such a way?

As he lay in bed during one particular hospital stay, he was silently shaking his fist at God due to the suffering that he was going through. Another boy in the same burn ward had a happy disposition, and Phil resented him for that. Why wasn't he angry and bitter as well? His positive outlook just rubbed salt in Phil's wounds.

Then one day Phil discovered that the other boy was receiving treatment for burns that he had received at the hand of his angry father. That's when the purifying conviction of the Holy Spirit touched Phil. Phil had a father who loved him and cared for him. He was angry and bitter because his own hand had precipitated an accident, whereas this boy was still happy even though his father had deliberately scalded him. So it was at age twelve that Phil realized this trial could either embitter him or refine his character. He challenged us that evening to decide whether bad things would make us "better or bitter." It's all based on our perspective of God's character.

It was as if the arms of Jesus wrapped themselves around me and I could hear his gentle whisper comforting me. He used the words of a member of the next generation to speak to the core of my soul and to soothe the pain of an entire community. Phil's commencement address became the stuff of legend, as students still reminisced about it years later.

In retrospect, Phil's story is also an illustration of how Millennials can serve as lifestyle mentors to those around them—including the adults in their lives. As I had unknowingly done with Kevin, Phil provided an example of a Christian response to unexpected tragedy and, in doing so, became a contemporary mentor to hurting people.

I had served as a coaching mentor (discussed in chapter 8) for Phil by providing encouragement, motivation, and guidance to meet the frightening challenge of giving his salutatorian address. In turn, Phil blessed my soul with the words he spoke that day. This experience reaffirmed the truth that, in a healthy adult-to-Millennial relational connection, the adult can benefit as much as the young person.

In Kevin's case, I had served as a contemporary mentor by modeling leadership and wisdom from afar. Kevin and I had never sat down and discussed the lessons that were taught during the senior trip, but he "caught" the lessons by watching the actions of an adult he respected. Years later, when Kevin told me of the impact of my passive mentoring, this served as another reminder that the contemporary model of mentoring is a style that every genuine Christian should embrace.

Scripture speaks to the importance of contemporary modeling as well. The apostle Paul exhorted the church in Philippi to model their lives after his: "Whatever you have learned or received or heard from me, or seen in me—put it into practice. And the God of peace will be with you" (Philippians 4:9). The words of the writer to the Hebrews further reinforce the importance of lifestyle mentoring for those in leadership roles: "Remember your leaders, who spoke the word of God to you. Consider the outcome of their way of life and imitate their faith" (Hebrews 13:7).

Dare to Be a Daniel

Historical mentoring models essentially do what contemporary models do, but they do it through the legacy they've left behind.[3] As in the example of Vernard Gant, historical models may be as recent as Dr. King and as long gone as Nehemiah.

Two other wonderful biblical models that can serve as historical mentors for the Millennial generation are Daniel (see Daniel 1–12) and Joseph (see Genesis 37–50). Here were genuine heroes, young men who stood for righteousness while they were yet teenagers. Let's explore each of their stories and note the parallels to today's youth culture.

Daniel lived without compromise in a culture similar to our post-modern world, which celebrates compromise in the guise of tolerance. He obeyed God's Word regardless of the possible consequences. When his homeland was conquered by an invading power and he was deported, he was among the young men selected for three years of training in preparation for entering the king's service. Daniel, however, was a young man of principle and courage; he and three Hebrew companions decided not to defile themselves with the royal food and wine, but to maintain a diet of vegetables and water (see Daniel 1). God honored their courage and commitment; when Daniel and his friends proved healthier than all the rest, the king ordered that every young man eat their diet.

What a marvelous example for a Millennial generation bombarded with the message, "You need to put yourself first. After all, don't you deserve it?" The concept of humbly obeying a higher authority is *not* the message that today's culture wants to sell to this upcoming generation. Daniel's name meant "God is my judge" and it is certainly evident that he knew the importance of putting God first in his life, whether it was a popular decision or not.

Another recorded episode not only reaffirms Daniel's commitment to principle but also demonstrates the importance he placed on maintaining communion with God. According to Daniel 6, he had so distinguished himself by his exceptional qualities that the king planned to set him over the whole kingdom. Daniel's enemies became so jealous that they attempted to find grounds for his dismissal. Listen to their strategy: "We will never find any basis for charges against this man Daniel unless it has something to do with the law of his God" (Daniel 6:5). Can you imagine such a statement being made by your enemies? What if the only thing they could find wrong with your life would be something to do with the law of your God? It's obvious that because of his spotless reputation Daniel must have been a contemporary mentor to many living in that time.

As happened earlier in his life, Daniel refused to compromise his principles. Nothing was going to usurp his priority of meeting with God. So, as was his custom, he continued to pray three times a day in front of open windows facing Jerusalem. If I were in Daniel's shoes, I think I would have come up with a variety of ingenious ways to hide the fact that I was praying, rather than risk my life. It cost Daniel a trip to the lions' den, where once again his faithful God came to the rescue.

Daniel unapologetically proclaimed the truth when the prevailing culture was openly hostile to that truth. Furthermore, Daniel *lived* the truth—the bottom line for the Millennial generation that wants authenticity in lives and not just words.

Joseph: Better, Not Bitter

Joseph also lived a life of conviction and unsurpassed integrity despite enduring many injustices, including being sold into slavery by his own brothers. As an Egyptian slave, he refused to give in to the sexual seduction of his master's wife, who then falsely accused him of attempted rape, which landed him in prison (see Genesis 39). Joseph did not let this terrible injustice make him bitter. He chose instead to become better, and he accepted this unfair imprisonment as the cost of obedience to God's commands.

Joseph's example is a pertinent message for Millennials who constantly hear the mantra that you can set your own standards and morality. You'll recall the dangerous consequence of this philosophy, as demonstrated in the story of the "lost children" of Rockdale County, recounted in chapter 3.

Joseph's story also provides an example of a young man who understood the importance of attempting to live a life from God's eternal perspective. When at last reunited with his brothers many years after being sold as a slave—and now in a powerful position that would have permitted him to punish them for their crime—Joseph said this to them: "As for you, you meant evil against me, but God meant it for good in order to bring about this present result, to preserve many people alive" (Genesis 50:20, NASB). This was the same lesson Phil learned after suffering through painful burns and skin grafts. And this is the lesson we all—young people and adults—must learn: the disappointments and trials in our lives are not simply evil inflicted upon us, but are situations that God can and will use to break us, to draw us to himself, and to accomplish his purpose.

Broken for True Blessing

This is not to say that the lessons of brokenness are ever easy. In his book *Shattered Dreams: God's Unexpected Pathway to Joy,* Larry Crabb contrasts the typical human reaction to disappointment and pain with God's desired result.

> People who find some way to deaden their pain
> never discover their desire for God in all its fullness.
> They'd rather live for relief and become addicts to
> whatever provides it. . . . Inconsolable pain, the kind

that drives away every vestige of happiness and renders us incapable of fully enjoying any pleasure, can be handled only by discovering a capacity for a different kind of joy. That is the function of pain, to carry us into the inner recess of our being that wants God. We need to let soul-pain do its work by experiencing it fully. . . . We need God. He is all we need. But until we realize that fact, we experience lesser desire as needs and devote our energy to arranging for their satisfaction.[4]

That very message—we need God and he is all we need—is one the Millennial generation needs to hear in the midst of a comfort-driven postmodern world.

In *The Sacred Romance,* Brent Curtis and John Eldredge refer to the "small dramas" that we construct and live in.[5] By "small dramas," they mean our dreams and aspirations that so often are shortsighted, shallow, or selfish. God, however, has a "grand story" in mind for each of us if we could only shift our perspective and see the bigger picture. The problem is that when we adults have lived small dreams, we cannot convey the grand story to the Millennial generation. And it is the grand story that they yearn to hear when they're confronted with humanly inexplicable tragedies, like 9-11, coupled with the shallowness of a culture shaped by a craving for status and comfort.

So what's the connection between brokenness and living God's grand story? In order to reshape our perspective and enable us to see the grand story, God often has to shatter our small dreams. The brokenness that results teaches us that God is not simply our "blesser" but our "lover." And it is this brokenness that the adult community must actually demonstrate to the Millennial generation before we can preach this truth with any credibility.

The process of brokenness encompasses three lessons. First, the absolute truth is *not* that God will make our lives easier, but that he will make them better. However, this better life is based on God's definition and not our own. We are empowered to draw close to God for one central purpose: to glorify him and to fully enjoy him forever. Second, when God seems most absent *from* us, he is doing his most important work *in* us. During these times of agony and loneliness he is yet at work to refine our character and conform us to his image. Often the shards of broken dreams around our feet are really the evidence of God chipping away at our carnal character in order to conform us to the image of his Son. Third, it isn't always good to be blessed with the good things of life. Bad times provide an opportunity to truly know God, which blessings in and of themselves never provide.[6]

Is such a message too painful and difficult to present to Millennials? Perhaps for some, but not for those who long to be authentic, to commit to a meaningful cause, and to make a difference in the world. What better cause can we present to this next generation than clearly teaching them about the real purpose in life: to glorify God and enjoy him forever? What better way to be genuine than by honestly letting them know that it's through the brokenness, pain, and tragedy that God produces a deep and authentic sacred romance? What better way to make a difference in this world than by committing to a genuine love affair with God that in turn will spread the "fragrance" of Christ to those who don't know him (see 2 Corinthians 2:14)?

Paul the Mentor

In closing, let's return to one of the great historic mentors of Scripture. The apostle Paul challenged the Corinthian Christians to take up the mantle of being lifestyle mentors by modeling their lives after his: "I urge you to imitate me. For this reason I am sending to you Timothy, my son whom I love, who is faithful in the Lord. He will remind you of my way of life in Christ Jesus, which agrees with what I teach everywhere in every church" (1 Corinthians 4:16-18). As implied in this passage, Paul had already authentically modeled for Timothy his devotion to Christ. Indeed, listen to his words to his protégé recorded in 2 Timothy 3:10-11: "You [Timothy], however, know all about my teaching, my way of life, my purpose, faith, patience, love, endurance, persecutions, sufferings—what kinds of things happened to me in Antioch, Iconium and Lystra, the persecutions I endured. Yet the Lord rescued me from all of them."

What better example than Paul of someone who modeled an authentic, mature devotion to Christ in the midst of brokenness and suffering. The passive mentoring that takes place when a Millennial watches an adult walk in God's presence during the bad times will have a far greater impact than any sermon he or she will ever hear. Our challenge as an adult generation is to follow Paul's example by letting the next generation know all about our teaching, way of life, purpose, faith, patience, love, endurance, persecution, and sufferings so that they will see a genuine romance with God—and then passionately want it for themselves.

CHAPTER SEVEN

Occasional Mentoring

LEVEL ONE: Passive Mentoring

- Contemporary Style
- Historical Style

LEVEL TWO: Occasional Mentoring

- Counseling Style
- Teaching Style
- Sponsoring Style

LEVEL THREE: Intensive Mentoring

- Discipling Style
- Spiritual Guiding Style
- Coaching Style

DURING MY TIME AS A SCHOOL PRINCIPAL IN LATIN AMERICA, I RECEIVED A telephone call one morning from an articulate and successful local businessman. Early in our conversation, I could sense a hint of desperation in his voice. Explaining that his son, Jeff (not his real name), had just been suspended from his private school due to academic failure, he wondered whether or not there was room in our school for additional applicants.

I very diplomatically told this father that our institution was primarily college preparatory in nature and that the academic climate was very rigorous, probably not the right fit for a student with a track record of poor academic performance. But he was not swayed by my rationale, not when he was so certain that this was a crossroad in his son's life, and our school was the boy's last chance to turn it around. Somewhat reluctantly, I arranged for an informal exploratory interview with him and his son the following day.

The next morning, Jeff and his father arrived half an hour before the scheduled interview. (This alone would have expressed the family's earnestness, given the fact that it is unusual in Latin America to arrive early for an appointment.) As I ushered Jeff and his father into my office, I noticed that Jeff had a hard time looking me in the eye. He seemed both depressed and emotionally downtrodden; either that, or he was hostile toward authority. It was too early to tell.

The father did most of the talking, though Jeff clearly indicated he wanted to be given another chance to succeed in school. However, his academic transcript confirmed my worst fears—he had earned failing grades across the board for his last semester. As we wound up the interview, I once more tried to gently explain that I thought our school was just not right for Jeff.

At that moment, the father burst into tears. "Mr. Egeler, can you do just one more thing for me? I would like you to call Jeff's previous principal before you make any decision." Still a bit stunned by the entire episode, I agreed.

As it turned out, Jeff's former principal was very familiar with our school. After we discussed the particulars, including Jeff's poor study habits and lack of motivation, he concluded, "In nearly every case, I would say that the student would have no chance for success in a competitive academic environment. But I think Jeff's case is special."

"What exactly do you mean?" I asked.

"Well," he said, "I perceive that Jeff needs an environment where he'll be challenged *and* where adults will genuinely care about him. If I were asked to describe your school's climate in one sentence, that's the description I would provide. So, something inside me really believes that your school is the right fit for Jeff. He is a very bright young man, even though his grades don't demonstrate it. I think this may be his last chance to succeed and to find his path in life."

When I hung up the telephone, that last comment replayed over and over in my mind: "I think this may be his last chance to succeed and to find his path in life." Those were practically the same words Jeff's father had used when he first spoke to me. That morning, I decided to take a risk and put my credibility on the line to champion Jeff's admission. Later that week, the admission committee agreed to admit Jeff based on my recommendation.

When I phoned Jeff's father with the news, he was ecstatic. I told him Jeff would need to sign an academic probationary contract that would outline measurable achievement goals. I wanted Jeff to know that it was a privilege to attend our school and that with this privilege came responsibility. Fortunately, when he and his father came in to sign the paperwork, Jeff seemed very positive about the new challenge.

Begging for One More Chance

It so happened that Jeff was an avid soccer player, and he indicated that he planned to try out for the varsity team. He had not played competitively before, so I tried to make sure his expectations were realistic. On the first day of tryouts, Jeff arrived late, dressed in jeans and not wearing soccer shoes. I pulled him aside and gently told him that in the future he needed to arrive on time, dressed to work hard. This was my first hint that the discipline and rigor of a competitive athletic team was completely foreign to Jeff.

But as tryouts concluded, it was readily apparent that we had a diamond in the rough: Jeff was an intense competitor and had good fundamental soccer skills and a nose for scoring goals. He had earned a spot on the roster. He even surprised everyone by gaining a starting position.

Nevertheless, Jeff was still on a learning curve. As the team was in the locker room preparing for our first game, he burst into my office in a panic. "Coach! Coach!" he said, "I forgot my uniform socks! I thought I could wear my personal socks."

"Well," I said, "there's not much we can do right now, so you'll just have to wear what you brought." As the team jogged out to the field a few minutes later, everyone was neatly dressed in the full uniform with maroon socks—except Jeff. He was wearing bright yellow ones!

By the middle of the season, it was obvious Jeff had begun to buy into the discipline and hard work required for success—he was one of our leading scorers. However, it became apparent that I had another issue on my hands: Jeff had an anger problem smoldering just below the surface. The combination of this and his competitive intensity made for a combustible mixture that would quickly burst into flame at the slightest provocation.

This was dramatically brought home during a game against one of our arch rivals. Recognizing that Jeff was a scoring threat, the opposing coach made sure his defender covered Jeff as tightly as possible. During one particularly competitive confrontation, Jeff felt that the defender had deliberately tripped him—yet, the referee did not call a foul, and play continued. I watched nervously as Jeff got up and ran toward the defender. These were the type of situations in which his temper had gotten him in trouble in the past, but this time it appeared he had everything under control—that is, until the defender tripped him a second time, and then seemed to laugh.

Jeff snapped. He chased the defender twenty yards across the field, dragged him down from behind, grabbed him by the neck, and started choking him while fans looked on in horror. I shot off our bench and sprinted across the field to pull Jeff off the other player. When Jeff saw the anger in *my* eyes, he immediately came back to reality and was mortified. The referee pulled out a red card and expelled Jeff from the game. With this expulsion, Jeff had to head to the locker room—and the team had to compete with one less player.

After the game, I found Jeff huddled in a corner of the locker room. I could tell that he had been crying. When I approached, he looked up and said in a haunting voice, "Coach, please don't say anything. I know what I did was wrong. I know I'm on probation. I know I've got a problem with anger and I need help. I'm just begging for one more chance."

I sat down in silence and pondered this earnest request. I had stuck my neck out for Jeff and was still smarting from the public humiliation my reputation had suffered with his display of aggression on the field. My perception was that every parent in the stands knew who Jeff was and that he was in school based on my recommendation. A part of me wanted to lash out and ask if this was how he demonstrated his gratitude.

But I also knew Jeff was just a kid and that a huge spiritual struggle was taking place deep within his soul. I knelt down beside him, hugged him, and promised that together we would deal with his anger.

I arranged for Jeff to see the school counselor, and slowly he began to flourish—in school, on the soccer field, and in his personal life. Even so, the counselor informed me that, because of some deep-seated issues, we needed to look at Jeff's healing as a long-term process.

Healing Prayers

During Jeff's senior year, he came into my office with a request. He was nearing the end of the counseling (which now had spanned several years), and he was due to enter into a final session of "healing prayers" in which he would spend several hours with two adults while confronting each sin and hurt in his life. This was typically a spiritually intense time.

The counselor usually would reserve the chapel for such a session so that a wooden cross would be available on which to symbolically nail every sin and hurt. Each person involved in these healing prayers would come to the session with the hurts and sins written on slips of paper as well as corresponding promises of God's provision and deliverance. During several hours of prayer and Scripture reading, he or she would post each piece of paper to the cross upon turning the hurt and sin over to the Savior. Because this was a form of spiritual warfare, the counselor would ask each of his clients to select another adult to join the session so that he or she would have support and additional prayer coverage. The second adult would need to be someone who the client trusted completely and who would be involved in follow-up after the session. As you may have guessed by now, Jeff had chosen me.

The unusual part of Jeff's request was that he wanted his healing prayers to take place in my office. We'd had many, many meetings in my office over the last several years, and it must have seemed a safer and more familiar place than the chapel. The counselor arranged to have a small wooden cross brought into my office, and I blocked out an entire morning to meet with Jeff and the counselor.

The prayer time was intense. We waded through the muck and mire of the strongholds that Satan had established in Jeff's life, and I began to fully grasp why he had been such an angry young man. It was a special privilege to see the miracle of the cross lifting the burdens off Jeff's back and watching them fall at the feet of Jesus. Jeff never looked back after that day. It truly was a turning point for him.

The story I've recounted is lengthy—and I've given only the highlights—yet it exemplifies the many interchanges that occur in the process of occasional mentoring. With this level of mentoring, the intentionality and intensity of the relationship between the protégé and the mentor is more significant than when mentoring on the passive level.

In Jeff's case, the specific style of occasional mentoring utilized was counseling. Both the school counselor and I provided timely advice and a correct perspective on viewing self, others, circumstances, and ministry. What's more, the mentoring was *intentional* (both the counselor and I worked with Jeff to address specific areas in his life that needed help) and *intense* (we had to invest time and energy into the relationship rather than the protégé simply watching from afar).

Kathy's Example

Consider Kathy's approach as another example of effective counselor mentoring, especially among Millennials. She taught health at the high school level and designed the curriculum around the primary objective of teaching students to make healthy lifestyle choices from a biblical perspective. One of her techniques was to have her students journal during the first five minutes of each class period about their lives and the decisions they were making. The students then handed in their journals at the end of each week. This time of daily reflection became a powerful medium of personal expression for quite a number of them.

There was something about the anonymity of journaling that seemed to provide the platform for these Millennial kids to open up and share confidential information with their teacher. With this development, however, Kathy needed to establish some protocol. Working with the counseling department, she developed guidelines for handling confidential information shared in journal entries. Two key principles were included in the protocol: first, if a student divulged information that could be deemed life threatening, Kathy would report this information immediately to the appropriate person to handle such a crisis; second, if a student divulged information serious enough to warrant outside counsel, Kathy would ask the student's permission before seeking advice from someone else.

The fear was that, once these two guidelines were implemented, students would shy away from sharing personal information. In fact, just the opposite happened. Kathy earned a measure of credibility, and students began to share their deepest secrets in their journal entries because they knew it was a safe way to seek help for sensitive issues. In time, Kathy developed a rich ministry by becoming an "initial" counselor for the counseling department. And after she had gained a student's permission to go to the next step, she would work closely with whichever counselor provided professional advice.

Seize Eternity

The second type of occasional mentoring is the "teacher." In this style the mentor strives to empower the protégé through the knowledge and understanding of a particular subject. A teacher mentor must have a level of mastery in a particular subject as well as the ability to convey that knowledge and understanding. This combination can be a dynamic tool to shape young lives.

Rob clearly was gifted with just such a combination. He taught upper-level high school English and was characterized not only by his high expectations of students but also by his warm and tender heart. It was through the study of literature that he wanted to help kids think critically while living with an eternal perspective.

A group of juniors came into Rob's class one day talking about the movie *Dead Poets Society,* a film in which Robin Williams portrays a passionate English teacher (Mr. Keating) at a New England prep school who challenges his students to seize the day (the Latin *carpe diem*) and thereby make their lives extraordinary. The plot culminates when one of the central characters, Neil, commits suicide as a result of the tension raised between wanting to follow his own dream (encouraged by Mr. Keating) and wanting to honor his father's dreams. He had concluded that the only way out of this dilemma was to take his own life. Though Mr. Keating had proven an excellent teacher mentor in many ways, because he did not believe in absolutes, he was incapable of providing clear and direct guidance when Neil needed it most. Ultimately, it was Neil's task to figure it out for himself—and it was a task for which he had no foundation to work from. Furthermore, Mr. Keating's admonition to *"carpe diem"* has a ring of truth to it, but not the entire truth.

Motivated by Rob's teaching and personal example, his students decided to print T-shirts that expressed the whole truth. The slogan they came up with was "Carpe Aeternitatem: Seize Eternity—Why Settle for Just a Day?" It is true that sometimes we can simply live in the past or in the future and miss out on embracing the present. However, these students reminded us that authentic Christians should not stop at simply seizing the moment. Instead, we should go further and "seize eternity."

Hebrews 12:1-2 urges us to maintain this eternal focus when the author states,

> Therefore, since we are surrounded by such a great cloud of witnesses, let us throw off everything that hinders and the sin that so easily entangles, and let us run with perseverance the race marked out for us. Let us fix our eyes on Jesus, the author and perfecter of our faith, who for the joy set before him endured the cross, scorning its shame, and sat down at the right hand of the throne of God.

Rob not only challenged his students to think eternally, but he went further and challenged them to bring this eternal perspective to their daily lives. As he unleashed their potential, the kids picked up the baton and served as peer mentors to their classmates by wearing their T-shirts one day every week for the rest of the school year.

Soccer Sermonettes

As a school administrator, I prayed God would provide just the right mentoring style for each student through the unique gifting he had given to each teacher. What passions could you use to intersect with a Millennial and thereby invest in his or her life? What opportunities do you have to interact regularly with a Millennial, which could then provide a platform to foster a mentoring relationship? Carefully evaluate your personal experience, personality, passions and interests, expertise, and gifting, and then look for ways to use these to invest in the lives of young people. In this way, you can impact the life of a Millennial as a school teacher, an employer, a Sunday school teacher, a youth group sponsor, a coach, or simply a friendly adult in the neighborhood.

It wasn't until I began working with Jeff that I realized I was not fully utilizing the platform that coaching soccer afforded. I learned very quickly that kids in Latin America do not suffer fools gladly when it concerns their national sport. Because I knew the game so well, I earned a measure of credibility with many young men in the same way Rob and Kathy earned credibility with their students.

When Jeff joined the team, it struck me that I was not being intentional about teaching biblical principles in my coaching. I had come from a public school environment in the United States where I was sensitive to the plurality of religious views. As such, I was adept at utilizing a contemporary model of mentoring in which I counted on my lifestyle to demonstrate God's truth. Obviously, I could and *should* do much more in a Christian school context.

As a result, I planned a series of soccer sermonettes (the expression I coined) for the start of varsity practices. I had typically established, printed, and posted a theme and schedule for each of the first ten practices leading up to the first game of the season. With my new mentoring initiative, I scheduled four separate sermonettes into the practice sequence. I was quite nervous before the first sermonette.

How would eighteen high school boys respond to giving up practice time to have Coach preach to them? Would their eyes just glaze over while they politely pretended to give me their attention? Would they actually go so far as to show me a lack of respect?

Showing Kindness to the Enemy

Deciding to speak to the issue of controlling one's competitive fire (with Jeff especially in mind), I told the following story from my own soccer experience, while weaving in a spiritual lesson.

As a college sophomore, I was in the midst of a breakout year in which I was leading the nation in scoring for small colleges. Midway through the season, we traveled to Long Island to play one of our arch rivals, a liberal arts college that had a high-powered soccer program with a roster of players on full athletic scholarships.

It was one of those games where you find yourself in a zone and it seems you can do nothing wrong. In the first half, I managed to free myself from the tight man-to-man marking for three shots on goal. All three shots were perfectly placed and I scored each time. The opposing goalkeeper was a freshman who had been a high school All-American, and I could tell that he was losing his composure by the time I scored the third goal. He began screaming at his defenders and demanding that they stop me—even if it meant "taking me out." When I heard these comments, it just got my own competitive juices flowing all the more.

Much like Jeff, I also had a competitive fire raging inside me that sometimes threatened to consume me. During halftime, I could sense this fire burning brighter. My desire was to go out in the second half and attempt to embarrass the opposing goalkeeper, even though deep in my heart I knew this was wrong. However, the goalkeeper had other ideas.

Early in the second half, he charged out of the goal, and feigning an attempt to go for the ball, he bowled me over from behind and ground me into the turf. I was awarded a penalty kick. Seething with anger, I deliberately struck the ball as hard as I could and shot it straight at the goalkeeper, intending to hurt him. Because this is not the normal penalty kick tactic, I caught him by surprise and the ball struck him in the chest without giving him a chance to react. Though I tried to score on the rebound, by then he had recovered and picked up the ball just before I got to it. I'll never forget the split-second when I saw the look of anger mixed with anticipation on his face as I was lying on my back and he had the ball clasped to his chest. Then he fell (actually he jumped!) on top of me and began punching me with his free hand. Suddenly, a big scrum developed around the two of us, with players pushing and shoving each other. Several players, including one of my defenders, were tossed out of the game.

During the ensuing confusion, I went to the corner of the field and completely lost control of my emotions. As I stood sobbing, the referee came over and asked if I needed a few more minutes to bring myself under control before he restarted the game. By this time, I was mortified at having become a public spectacle, so I quickly tried to pull myself together.

When we opened the season the next year against the same college, I was absolutely focused on payback. Early in the game, I managed to beat the defense on a breakaway, and instead of attempting to just tuck the ball away into the net, I dribbled past the goalkeeper to humiliate him. After I pushed the ball into the net, I ran back to him and spoke a few choice words. This was something I had never done before or since, and it caught me off guard. After the game, I was incredibly ashamed. I began to wonder if I could really compete at a high level and retain my Christian testimony. How was a Christian athlete supposed to compete without this type of anger welling up inside?

I asked God for guidance, ready to give up the sport if that's what it took. Needless to say, my coach was a little unnerved by this line of thinking. After several weeks of anguish, the Holy Spirit impressed upon me to apply Proverbs 25:21-22 to my situation: "If your enemy is hungry, give him food to eat; if he is thirsty, give him water to drink. In doing this, you will heap burning coals on his head, and the LORD will reward you." In other words, demonstrate kindness to your enemies—or in my case, to my soccer opponents.

I knew that one particularly fast and physical defender was likely to be assigned to cover me all over the field during our next game against this same college from Long Island. As with the goalkeeper, there was certainly no love lost between he and I. Yet when he made a nice tackle and stripped me of the ball, I complimented him. This so unnerved him that he interpreted my remark as a new level of trash talking. He spat at me. I was furious that my good intentions were being repaid with evil, but the Holy Spirit reminded me of my ultimate objective. So I complimented him a second time and he gave me a quizzical look. The third time I complimented him, he responded by saying, "You really mean that, don't you?"

When we played this team again, a strange thing happened—we began to regularly compliment each other. Instead of our performances suffering, we spurred each other on as iron sharpens iron. By the end of the season, our teams met in the playoffs, and we managed to beat them in overtime. Afterward, my coach approached me as I was preparing to change and said, "Your man-to-man marker wants to meet with you outside."

I didn't know what to expect, especially as this guy's college soccer career had just come to an end with such a disappointing defeat. He asked, "Do you remember that game where you complimented me and I turned and spit at you? Why did you do that?" I explained that I was a Christian and that I had been convicted to change my approach to competition.

He listened intently, then just shook his head and responded, "Man, I've got to tell you that whatever you did worked. What we experienced this season was the best and purest form of competition I've ever known. I can't pretend to understand what you're describing in terms of your faith, but whatever you've got, don't ever lose it." With that, he reached out and gave me a hug, and then disappeared back into the visitors' locker room.

I lingered outside for a moment and the words of Proverbs came back to me: "In doing this, you will heap burning coals on his head, and the LORD will reward you." The Lord had answered my cry for help in a time of need; I had implemented his guidance with fear and trembling, and he had rewarded me.

When I finished telling this sermonette to the eighteen young men in front of me, they just sat in stunned silence. I knew I had struck a chord. After I had dismissed them, one of the players, who was injured and on crutches, approached me and asked, "Coach, can you tell me when the next sermonette will be?" When I asked why he wanted to know, he said, "Because I'm going to make sure that my mom schedules my doctor's appointment so that I don't miss practice that day."

As I walked to my office, I regretted that I had waited this long to be more intentional in becoming a teacher mentor to my soccer players. But I also knew I wouldn't waste any more opportunities in the future.

And Now a Word About Sponsors

The final type of occasional mentoring is the "sponsor." In this style the mentor strives to empower the protégé through career guidance as he or she matures and develops. This necessitates a mentor's ability to discern gifting and ability, then to help maximize those talents in the protégé.

Dr. Jim Allen, senior vice president of HCJB World Radio in Latin America, traveled extensively while representing that ministry, but he placed a high priority on being in town for an important weekly meeting with several high school boys. These young men were interested in possibly becoming preachers someday—hence their nickname, the "preacher boys."

In addition to his duties with HCJB, Jim served as the pastor for the local English-speaking church. His goal was that each of these young men—his protégés—would eventually participate in conducting an entire evening service at the church. Every week, they would study the Scriptures, and Jim would help them prepare for the varying responsibilities they would need to handle. He would have the young men assume small responsibilities in services, leading up to the full evening service. This was less threatening and allowed Jim to nurture their development a step at a time.

On the nights the guys went solo, people needed to arrive early to find a seat. It wasn't because the preaching was so profound, but because the entire community was eager to support these fledgling preachers. These were always amazing services, in large part because they provided such a clear-cut example of what one man's investment in the next generation could produce. Several of these Millennials have gone on to fulfill their dreams of serving in full-time ministry as a result of the investment Pastor Jim made in their lives.

Peter's Mountain

The son of missionary parents, Peter was an undersized, competitive, and hardworking goalkeeper during his high school career. He went on to college in the United States on a soccer scholarship. When he graduated, he dreamed of returning to Latin America to pursue a professional soccer career. This was going to be a tall mountain to climb, as the professional soccer scene was highly competitive—especially for foreigners like Peter.

Before Peter's folks left for a yearlong furlough in North America, his mother asked me whether or not we should try to discourage Peter's plans, thinking that he might be pursuing a pipe dream. Perhaps the appropriate counsel would have been to advise him to get on with his life by preparing for a more realistic career. Yet I felt that this was a time in Peter's life when he should be encouraged to shoot for the stars and pursue his dreams, no matter how unrealistic they might appear. I didn't want him to look back one day and wonder "if only."

Peter's first challenge was to establish a residence because his folks were spending the year in North America. Given the fact that he was right out of college, he really didn't have the financial resources to set up a house and live for several months without a stable income. But God miraculously provided.

Sarah, one of Peter's former teachers and the mother of one of his best friends, went out and bought lunch tickets for a semester so he would have at least one hot meal a day. And, because Peter had expressed a desire to possibly coach soccer one day, I allowed him to serve as my assistant coach in exchange for payment of his utility bills. With this arrangement, I received the benefit of getting excellent technical assistance for my goalkeepers and Peter received "free" electricity and a phone for his apartment. In addition, I also had an entire soccer season to invest in him so that I could nurture and guide him in this career path.

During the fall, Peter tried out for several professional soccer teams with no success. In each case, he was cut from the roster because he was a foreigner, and the league rule was that each team was only permitted two foreigners (and he was never one of the top two). When spring came, Peter was down to his last possible team, which was located in a small town several hours from the city.

Pleased with his performance at the first practice, Peter's hopes were immediately dampened when the coach informed him that he was bringing in another goalkeeper to compete for the roster spot. The new goalkeeper dominated the next day of tryouts, and Peter returned to his little hotel room with the realization that his dream was slipping away. He could not sleep that night, which was a problem because the next day would be his final chance to prove himself and he needed to be at his best.

Because he was awake, he decided to spend some time reading the Bible and praying. In the early hours of the morning, the Holy Spirit spoke to him very clearly and he fell to his knees before God. It was then that Peter surrendered his dream and told God that his will be done. Peter committed to serve God in whatever way he could— even if it meant giving up his dream of a professional soccer career.

A supernatural peace swept over him as he prepared for the morning practice, and even though he did his best, he knew he had absolutely no chance of making the team. However, when the coach revealed the final roster, Peter was stunned to hear his name called. Even from Peter's biased perspective, the other goalkeeper was far superior, yet the coach had chosen Peter, confirming to him that the hand of God was at work. This completely unexpected fulfillment of his dream (which Peter considered a minor miracle) served to reaffirm the commitment that he had made to serve God. When he humbly relinquished his dream, God gave it back to him.

Lifted Up to Lift Others

This powerful spiritual lesson simply underscored the conversations Peter and I had had a few months earlier when I had shared with him the truth I had learned from 1 Peter 5:6-7: "Humble yourselves, therefore, under God's mighty hand, that he may lift you up in due time. Cast all your anxiety on him because he cares for you." As a child, I had memorized this verse and often was sustained by its truth through my years of growing up in East Africa. As I matured, however, I learned that I needed to first humble myself under the mighty hand of God before I could truly cast my anxiety upon him.

I also learned that I needed to first humble myself under the mighty hand of God when it came to my lifelong dreams and aspirations. My personal ambition typically did not have an eternal perspective! The amazing thing, as I told Peter, was that God seemed to "lift me up in due time" when I turned my dreams and aspirations over to him. And, of course, that's exactly what happened to Peter as well.

In Peter's case, I functioned both as a sponsor mentor *and* a counselor mentor. As a sponsor mentor I provided career guidance by encouraging him to pursue his aspirations as a professional soccer player and eventually as a coach. And within the framework of those career dreams, I served as a counselor mentor by providing timely advice and a correct biblical perspective.

My relationship with Peter also illustrates that lines are often blurred in working with Millennials. Typically, an adult will not have only one mentoring style but will employ facets of several to meet the unique needs and potential of each protégé. The experience of working with Peter and of preaching my sermonettes were defining moments for me as a mentor, as I realized that the experiences God led me through could be shared with the Millennial generation.

As you continue to read through this book, my challenge to you is to reflect on what experiences God would have you share with Millennials in your circle of influence. You may have the same opportunity to "seize eternity."

CHAPTER EIGHT

Intensive Mentoring

LEVEL ONE: Passive Mentoring
- Contemporary Style
- Historical Style

LEVEL TWO: Occasional Mentoring
- Counseling Style
- Teaching Style
- Sponsoring Style

LEVEL THREE: Intensive Mentoring
- Discipling Style
- Spiritual Guiding Style
- Coaching Style

KAZUO OZAKI WAS ONE OF THE MOST EFFECTIVE "DISCIPLING" MENTORS I HAVE ever known. Kazuo left Japan with his family to serve in Latin America with HCJB World Radio, sacrificing much of his own culture and heritage for the sake of the gospel. His family immersed themselves in an English-speaking North American professional environment while living in a Spanish-speaking Latin American country. As a result, they had to learn two new languages. In addition, Kazuo's children were educated in an English-speaking school with a North American curriculum, so their Japanese culture and heritage became just one of three cultures woven into the fabric of their lives. Essentially, Kazuo's children grew up to be no longer "pure" Japanese.

In God's providence, this experience gained Kazuo a significant measure of credibility within the expatriate Japanese community. As Japanese parents looked for educational options for their children, the local international Christian school became their school of choice. And because these kids needed to master the English language to succeed academically, Kazuo stepped into the breach and began personally to serve as an English tutor for every Japanese Millennial. This was not a part of Kazuo's job description and it was extremely time consuming, but he saw it as a tremendous opportunity to make an investment in the lives of the next generation.

As Kazuo earned the respect and trust of these mostly unchurched young people, he began to lead many of them to a personal knowledge of Jesus Christ. In time, he established a Sunday school class for these students so that he could empower his new protégés by teaching them the basics of their newfound faith.

Along with the rest of us, Kazuo had learned that the month of May could be the worst of times at an international school. Things rush to their conclusion. Exams and final projects fill the hours for both faculty and students. May is also the time of saying good-bye—sometimes forever. But May could also be the best of times. One of my favorite activities was the annual May baptismal service, when the local English-speaking church would be packed as students from a variety of countries publicly proclaimed their commitment to Jesus Christ.

Kazuo was participating in the service this particular year because one of the students being baptized was a young lady whom he had led to the Lord and discipled. Though her parents were not Christians, she wanted them to be present *and* she wanted her mentor, Kazuo, to baptize her. It brought tears to my eyes as I watched Kazuo conduct his portion of the service in *three* languages — English for the benefit of the school community, Spanish for the benefit of the Latin American community, and Japanese for the benefit of the student's family. This young woman wanted to be sure her parents understood the full significance of her commitment.

For the Bumps Along Life's Road

Another style in intensive mentoring is the "spiritual guide." Rather than teaching a protégé the basics of following Christ as in the discipling style, this method empowers through accountability, direction, and spiritual insight, providing guidance for the inevitable bumps in life's road that a young person will confront.

Takashi was an example of a young man whose life was shaped by two mentors: Kazuo as a discipler and me as a spiritual guide. The son of Japanese immigrants, Takashi's parents sent him to our Christian school in the sixth grade. He enrolled with very little English comprehension, yet when he graduated seven years later he was the class valedictorian.

On the evening before the graduation ceremony, Takashi's mother invited a number of special guests for a Japanese meal in their home, among them Kazuo and me. There were three boys in the family and each one had invited me to a similar event. Takashi was the youngest of the three, and just a week before the dinner, we had spent some significant time together during his senior trip. As we had watched the sun set one evening, Takashi had shared with me his profound regret about the emotional distance he felt from his father. This was a common theme that I heard from the sons of international businessmen, particularly from cultures in which the father was expected to be the breadwinner and little else. Takashi ached for a more intimate relationship with his father; he saw the relationships that some of his friends had with their dads and he wanted that too.

With this in mind (and with Takashi's permission), at the end of the graduation dinner, I stood up to speak with Kazuo as interpreter at my side. Those listening were certainly a reflection of Takashi's life. The students there, including the missionary kid who introduced Takashi to Jesus, represented five different nationalities. There was also a handful of adults, including others besides Takashi's parents from the Japanese community.

As I began, my main intent was to help Takashi's mother and father see their son from my perspective, in hopes of introducing them to a side of his character of which they might have been unaware. With Kazuo translating my words into Japanese, I shared an experience that shaped Takashi's early spiritual formation, one in which I had served as his spiritual guide.

The Good Son

Takashi's older brother was going through a difficult period in his life and had decided to drop out of school. Because of the high value the Japanese community places on education, this was perceived as a shameful event for the family, and Takashi was just as upset and angry with his brother as their parents were.

I too was concerned with the long-term implications of a student dropping out of high school, so I developed a strategy to try to maintain some emotional ties with Takashi's older brother. Knowing that he was a gifted soccer player and that he loved the sport, I proposed that he continue to practice with the team even though he would not be eligible to compete in the games. Takashi's older brother was excited about this opportunity, but I told him I needed the permission of the soccer team before we could proceed.

At the conclusion of the next practice, I called all the athletes into a huddle and proposed my plan. This was a wonderfully mature group of young men, and they were more than happy to consent. Afterward, as the rest of the team members were embracing his older brother, I looked across the field and I saw Takashi, obviously very angry and hurt, scuffing the ground with his shoes. I went home that night with a heavy heart.

The next morning I called Takashi into my office. At the time, I was the school's chief administrator, so a conference with the director usually meant a very serious matter. Takashi nervously entered and asked, "Did you need to see me, Coach?"

"I sure do. Please take a seat. I want to read something to you." Then I opened my Bible to Luke 15 and simply read the story of the prodigal son. The Scriptures teach that the Word of God is sharper than any two-edged sword, and this truth was reaffirmed that day. When I finished the passage, I looked up and I saw the tears in Takashi's eyes. He stood up and said, "Don't say a word, Coach; don't say a word."

I pulled back the curtain in my office window and watched as Takashi headed toward the lockers where his older brother was sitting. Takashi walked over to his brother and embraced him. It was a moment in which the power of the gospel message was clearly on display—a power that transcended culture. The Holy Spirit had revealed to Takashi through Luke 15 that he was the "good son." Takashi had a tender heart toward the things of God, so he knew that God wanted him to welcome his older brother and not to harbor animosity and bitterness toward him. In obedience, he reached out to his older brother and "welcomed him home."

The Power of Reconciliation

As I finished the story, I told Takashi's father that he had a jewel for a son and that he needed to get to know him on a deeper level. By now, Takashi's father was weeping, his heart pierced by my message. A hush fell over the room and I could hear sniffling from some of Takashi's classmates as well.

Finally, one young girl from Taiwan ventured to ask, "Mr. Egeler, can we share too?" Of course I gave my assent and, one by one, each student shared from the heart. It was a beautiful moment. The last to speak was the friend who had introduced Takashi to Jesus. His voice was thick with emotion as he recalled an incident in which he and Takashi had disagreed and over which they had parted ways. Evidently, the relationship had never been fully restored. He stood up, walked over to Takashi, and said, "I've treated you poorly, Takashi, and you've responded with kindness. I want to ask for your forgiveness. I'm ashamed because I'm the older brother in Christ and should have been an example, but I failed. Will you forgive me?" At that moment, they embraced and were reconciled.

As we left that night, Takashi's father refused to bid good night with the traditional polite bow; instead, he reached over and embraced me with a warm hug. Kazuo pulled me aside afterward and asked, "Do you really know what happened tonight?" I shook my head no. He explained, "The couple that was invited from the Japanese community has never been around Christians. For them to see young people sharing authentically was more powerful than any preaching that I could have done."

Takashi gave his valedictory address the next night and began by sharing his personal testimony. Then, looking at his seated class-mates, he asked that his friend stand and be recognized for leading him to a saving knowledge of Jesus Christ. It was a marvelous moment—for two reasons. First, it would not have happened without the reconciliation the night before. Second, there was a hidden irony—Takashi was graduating first in the class but only a few people knew that his friend was graduating last in the class. I'm convinced, however, that at the judgment seat, Jesus is not going to ask for anyone's grade point average. Instead, he'll say, "Well done, my son, I introduced you to Takashi, and then you introduced him to me."

Takashi next told a story of the "modern prodigal son," inter-weaving his own life story with the Luke 15 Scripture. Finally, begging the audience's pardon, he switched to the language of his homeland. He thanked the entire Japanese community attending in support of their "favorite son," and thanked his parents for making both the financial and the cultural sacrifice to send him to this school. He told his parents that the greatest experience he had at the school was entering into a personal relationship with Jesus Christ, and he invited them to discover the same relationship.

He then concluded by speaking directly to his father, saying that he was afraid of slowly separating from him and that he wanted to rebuild their relationship. And with those words he told his father and mother that he loved them. What a moving experience not only for Takashi and his family, but for everyone in that auditorium whose lives were touched by the heart of this authentic, transparent Millennial.

More than Lunch

I met Greg when he served on our faculty as a high school Bible teacher. A youth pastor by training, he willingly retooled and learned the craft of an educator, feeling that the career switch gave him a better platform to intentionally mentor students. Now he enjoyed regular involvement in their lives rather than the sporadic and limited interaction he had as a youth pastor. Greg was always intentionally exploring ways to invest in young lives. He even developed the idea of establishing a fund with which to take young men out to lunch. If you know male teenagers, you know they never turn down a free lunch!

What set Greg's plan apart was that these meals were not times merely to have a casual conversation or to establish friendships. Greg targeted certain young men in his class, invited them out for lunch, and then was intentional about providing accountability, direction, and insight into their questions, commitments, and decisions.

The risk of going beyond a friendship level to being an adult in a Millennial's life paid off. These kids so yearned for this depth of communication and relationship that they eagerly responded to Greg's effort. But for this to happen, Greg needed to be intentional, to make a time (and financial) commitment, and to risk by going beneath the surface in a relationship with a young person.

The payoff was huge, however, as Greg became a spiritual guide to a generation of young men whose lives he pointed toward living in light of eternity. Greg has performed weddings, attended graduations and reunions, and stayed in contact with his protégés as they have made an effort to keep him in the loop of their lives. He was their spiritual guide.

Putting Feet to Faith

The final mentoring style in this intensive level is the "coach." The primary goal of the coach mentoring style is to provide motivation and impart skills and application to meet a task or challenge.

This mentoring style has some strong similarities to the sponsoring style highlighted in chapter 7. The key difference between the two is that coaching requires a heightened level of intentionality and intensity. Both styles have the overall goal of seeking to empower the protégé to maximize his or her gifts and talents for the glory of God; coaching simply requires a greater level of commitment for both the mentor and the protégé.

Greg also served as an example of a coach mentor with his involvement in the Christian Service Outreach (CSO) ministry, an extracurricular activity at the international Christian school in which students were given opportunities to "put feet to their faith" by becoming involved in practical ministry. The Millennials' propensity to voluntarily contribute their time toward what they feel are worthy endeavors was certainly borne out in the success of the CSO program. As a rule, 80 to 90 percent of the high school students would *voluntarily* sign up to be involved in CSO, even though the commitment normally involved a weekly meeting, ministry on weekends, and an annual ministry trip within the country.

In Greg's group the adults served primarily as advisors and the older students pretty much carried the ball in organizing and leading the ministry involvement. This was particularly true of the annual ministry trip to a small Indian village in the Amazon jungle. Every year, this group would go to the village and conduct in Spanish a week-long vacation Bible school for the children. The student leaders would plan, organize, and implement the entire trip; the adults would merely assist in the process.

As such, the adults became coaching mentors, providing motivation and imparting skills and application to do a specific task or meet a challenge. In order to nurture and develop student leaders, the adults would handpick underclassmen and then groom them to eventually fill leadership roles when they were ready to assume full responsibility as upperclassmen. In all honesty, it would have been easier for the adults to do the planning, organizing, and implementing for the ministry trip themselves. But, in doing so, they would have missed the opportunity to be coaching mentors to these young people.

A Risk and a Reward

As you might imagine, I have had numerous opportunities to serve as a coaching mentor in my role as the school's soccer coach. Typically blessed with one of the most competitive programs in the city, we had just completed a particularly successful season. But as I surveyed our lineup for the following year, I realized we had some major holes to fill.

The one critical position that needed to be addressed was the sweeper back. For those of you unfamiliar with soccer, this is the player who anchors the defense. The sweeper is responsible to communicate with the defenders in front of him; he's called a sweeper because he's expected to cover for and sweep up after others' mistakes. The athletic qualities that a coach looks for in a sweeper are speed, ball skill, intelligence, and good tackling ability (the ability to steal the ball from an opponent). Unfortunately, I did not have anyone this particular year that met all of these qualifications.

Before the season began, I called John into my office. He was tall and gangly, very bright, and had good tackling ability. However, he was slow and his ball skills were not quite what I wanted in a sweeper back. Still, John was the best available candidate. I sat him down across from me and carefully explained the role and my expectations of the position.

As I've mentioned, John was quite intelligent, so when I finished my explanation, his eyes widened and he said, "Coach, you're not thinking of putting me at sweeper back, are you?" And before I could answer, he said, "We both know it's probably a mistake because I'm not fast enough and my ball skills aren't that great."

"John," I said, "you're my best option. I'm willing to take the risk. I'm going to invest in you and we'll play to your strengths while minimizing your weaknesses." And with that commitment on my part, John took a deep breath and said yes.

We constructed the defense that year around John. I positioned him further back to compensate for his lack of speed and to carve out more time on the ball (more time for him to control the ball). We focused on maximizing his intelligence as we went with a particular defensive scheme that relied on quick reads. And, thanks to the team coming together as a cohesive unit, we were remarkably successful. The risk of placing John at sweeper seemed to be paying off.

Late in the season, we had a game against one of the city's

powerhouse teams. They had a superb attacking player who was an apprentice professional (he would be playing professional soccer in a year or two). Against all odds, we were tied at halftime and I could hardly catch my breath in the excitement. As my players sat on the grass, I reminded them that the only reason we had been successful during the season was because we had bonded together and each player had been willing to sacrifice individual success for the good of the team. I used the first half as an illustration: We had no business even being on the field with this team; their substitutes were better than our top starters. Yet we were in the game because we were playing together—eleven players as one.

As I ended my halftime comments, I said, "It's inevitable that the superstar forward is going to break through this second half. I'm going to instruct John to go in for the tackle when he breaks through. We all know that John cannot keep up with him, so I want to utilize John's tackling ability and rely on the element of surprise. I'm telling you this now so that we're in this together." The risky tactic I was proposing was asking John to attempt to steal the ball rather than delaying the forward until another defender could catch up to help. Because the sweeper is the last man between the attacker and the goalkeeper, he gives up a breakaway if he misses the tackle.

As John stepped onto the field for the second half, I put my arm around him and whispered in his ear, "John, I've got confidence in you." He just shook his head; I knew he had butterflies in his stomach.

Late in the second half, the score was still tied. Sure enough, the superstar forward broke through the defense and was running right at John in an attempt to beat him one-on-one. Fearing the worst, I was tempted to drop my head and close my eyes. However, John stood tall and carefully gauged the opposing forward. Just as he made his move,

John timed his tackle perfectly, slid in, and won the ball. The forward flew over the top of John with a shocked look on his face. John got up with the ball, made his outlet pass, and looked over to me with a huge smile on his face. I smiled back and gave a big thumbs-up. Though our team ended up losing the game in the waning moments, I sensed that John and his teammates had won something far greater.

When I left Latin America, I was reminded of the impact I had made on John as his coaching mentor. On hearing of my departure, he wrote a long e-mail and reminded me that I had taken the risk to provide him an opportunity to meet a huge challenge. He told me I had taught him invaluable lessons about leadership, motivation, encouragement, and persistence. My belief in him and my willingness to allow him to strive for more than what he believed possible had impacted his life forever. Now, he said, he is looking to do the same for the generation coming up behind him.

As I've said all along, that's the beauty and the power of mentoring: passing on the baton to the next generation, who will then take it and hand it off to the generation after it.

CHAPTER NINE

Mentoring Lessons:
The Barnabas Model

THE STORY OF BARNABAS PROVIDES A RICH RESERVOIR OF WISDOM AND INSIGHT for aspiring mentors. His touch on the lives of two early church leaders, Paul and John Mark, has had a profound impact over the centuries, as illustrated by the fact that fourteen of the twenty-seven books of the New Testament were written by protégés of Barnabas. Could it be that if Barnabas had not embraced his ministry of mentoring we might be missing half of the New Testament today?

The lessons we glean from his life are also especially relevant to mentoring the Millennial generation. John Mark was obviously a member of the next generation; Paul, Barnabas's other protégé, took the baton and also invested in a member of the next generation—Timothy.

Traveling with Barnabas

We first meet Barnabas in Acts 4:36-37. Apparently, the name Barnabas was a nickname (meaning "Son of Encouragement") given to him by the apostles. This episode shows him to be a generous man who sold his land to bless the church's needy—quite a contrast to

Ananias and Sapphira, who also sold their land to give to the poor, but deceptively withheld some of the money for themselves. The result for them was deadly—literally! (See Acts 5:1-11.)

The mentoring lesson we can take from this is that Barnabas had a pure heart; he genuinely wanted to encourage others, without any selfish motives. As such, a true mentor who wants to impact the next generation will not seek personal benefit or recognition from a mentoring relationship. His or her sole motive is to contribute to the kingdom of God.

Acts 6–7 is pivotal in setting the stage for Barnabas's ministry, because it is here that we glean some insight into the risk he took by accepting Saul (later known as Paul) as a protégé. Saul could rightly be called the leading religious terrorist of his day; he witnessed and openly approved of the stoning of Stephen, an early church leader. Indeed, seeing this godly man persecuted and killed only made him more intent to destroy the church (see Acts 8:1-2).

Then the unimaginable happened: Saul professed to have become a Christian and began preaching in Damascus. Later, when he arrived in Jerusalem, the disciples were afraid of him, unsure of his true motives (see Acts 9:26). In all likelihood, their perception was that Saul was using this conversion experience as a ruse to further infiltrate the church. Indeed, how would we respond if our greatest enemy proclaimed that he had converted to Christianity?

This is when Barnabas entered the picture. Seeing past the rough edges and the potential danger, he willingly took Saul under his wing. Barnabas discerned Saul's sincerity and authenticity because he had "mentor's eyes"—the ability to see potential in a person and the willingness to assume short-term risk. The mentoring steps Barnabas took in this case included (1) taking time to check out Saul's story; (2)

discerning Saul's potential; (3) linking or bridging between Saul and the apostles; and (4) risking his own reputation among the apostles by speaking on Saul's behalf.[1]

In Acts 11:22-30, we see the balance between Barnabas's more public, large-group exhorting ministry and his more intensive personal mentoring with Saul. After a period of ministering in Antioch and seeing its great potential for receiving the gospel, Barnabas did not assume he could do it all. Instead, he saw a fit between Saul's gifts and abilities and the needs in Antioch. Serving as a "divine contact," he thrust Saul into a context where his apostolic call to reach the Gentiles had an opportunity to flourish.

Let's move ahead to Acts 12:25–13:3, a passage that briefly explains how Barnabas brought into the mix a second protégé—his nephew John Mark. Obviously, Barnabas had the ability to spot emerging younger leaders as well as emerging older ones! The same potential he discerned in the life of Saul, he saw in the life of a member of the next generation. (There are times when you may be the *only* one to see that potential. But it just may be that you are the one person God has selected to step into the life of a young person to make an impact for eternity.)

Though the rest of Acts 13 does not appear to disclose much about mentoring on the surface, a significant lesson is presented nevertheless. Early in the passage, the order of the names reads "Barnabas and Saul"; but by the end of the passage, the order has been reversed. This reversal seems to indicate that at the beginning of the first missionary journey Barnabas was the team leader, but gradually, Saul took over that role. In their book *Barnabas, Encouraging Exhorter: A Study in Mentoring,* Laura Rabb and Bobby Clinton call this an "authority switch."[2]

The mentoring lesson here is that the protégé may at some point surpass his or her mentor, at which time the mentor must step aside to allow further development. In India, there is an expression, "Nothing grows under a banyan tree."[3] A banyan is a particularly leafy tree so large that it does not allow sunlight to penetrate its branches. Hence, it is also especially difficult for any vegetation to grow under its shadow. In the same way, a mentor can keep the sunlight (recognition, acclaim, or opportunities) from shining on his or her protégé. This can happen intentionally (due to jealousy, personal insecurity, or desire for control) or unintentionally (due to ignorance). However, like Barnabas with Saul, effective mentors will rejoice when their protégés eventually exceed them. If we are to be effective mentors, we will demonstrate the same humility with our protégés.

In Acts 15:36-41, we find a mentor's heart colliding with a visionary's passion. Barnabas was equally committed to Paul's vision, but he saw the implementation of the vision with mentor's eyes. For Barnabas, developing harvest workers was as important as reaping the harvest. Paul saw John Mark's abandonment of their first mission as a major failure and was adamant that he not accompany them on another. Barnabas and Paul parted ways over the conflict—Barnabas moved by a mentor's compassion and Paul moved by a missionary's passion. Years later, however, Paul indirectly affirmed Barnabas's restorative work with John Mark when he commented on how useful Mark was to him in his ministry (see 2 Timothy 4:11).

From this incident Barnabas teaches us the importance of forgiveness and restoration when a protégé repents and seeks to get back on his or her feet. Whenever possible, a mentor should avoid the temptation to "leave the wounded behind."

You Never Know Who's Watching

During our years in Latin America, our two older children decided they would sign up to play youth baseball along with many of their friends from other expatriate families. Though they were initially placed on a team coached by a parent from our school, due to an administrative glitch they were "traded" to a team coached by parents who were total strangers. The kids were upset and begged me to let them quit, but I wanted to teach them a lesson about honoring and following through on a commitment—even though I was as ticked as they were! And when I showed up at their first couple of practices, I somewhat reluctantly got roped into helping coach (you know how that goes!).

By the end of the season, I had begun to develop an excellent relationship with the other two coaches. One of them was Bob, an international businessman. We would get together over a cup of coffee each week and commiserate over our mounting losses (our team was not very competitive!). At the end of the season, we had a barbecue at Bob's house and as my wife and I were preparing to leave, Bob asked, "Say, Dan, what is the philosophy of education at your school?"

Because we were serving at a Christian school, I knew that this answer would take a bit of time. We called the baby-sitter to tell her we were going to be late, and we spent the next several hours discussing our faith and its application to our lives. The next week Bob called and asked if he and his wife could come over so that I could "teach them how to pray." Having never been asked that question before, I was a bit dumbfounded at first—but of course I said yes.

It was on that visit that Bob told me he had been watching me closely, because he had the perception that Christians were just a bunch of aggressive "Bible thumpers." This was the first indication that I had been serving as a passive mentor to him. Bob's experience had been that anyone who embraced the claims of Christ did so only during moments of weakness or crisis. In other words, Christianity was simply a crutch for weak people who needed help to get through life.

Bob admitted that he was going through a difficult time in his business, and he *did not* want to resort to religion to help him get through a rough patch in his life. Despite this fact, Bob clearly confessed to a deep-seated spiritual void in his soul. I prayed with him at the end of our time and gave him a Bible as he left. I told him that his assignment was to read the four Gospels three times each before scheduling our next meeting.

Bob called a week later and told me he had completed his assignment. When we met in my office, I could tell he was under the conviction of the Holy Spirit and minutes later he accepted the gift of salvation. As we concluded our time together, Bob asked if I would pray for him now that he was a child of God. He wanted to be sure the seed sown in his life had landed in good soil and would have a chance to grow to maturity. I put my arm around him and prayed a short prayer of blessing as I'd done countless times before. But this time was different. When I opened my eyes, Bob was standing with his arms outstretched and he was shaking.

"What's the matter?" I asked.

Bob kept his eyes closed and answered, "Have you ever taken drugs, Dan?"

"I can't really say that I have, Bob. Why?"

He went on to explain that he felt like he had just been injected with a giant shot of Novocain and could feel a healing power flow from my arm through his body. Most importantly, it touched his soul. His lifelong ache was gone and he now felt whole.

Childlike Trust

Bob and I met regularly for several months and it was amazing to watch him grow in his faith. Even though I served as *his* discipler, Bob was an incredible encouragement to me as I observed an intimacy with God and childlike trust that I seemed to lack in my own life.

Once, during this time, Bob sold a car and then found out that the vehicle identification number on the registration was incorrect. In this Latin American country, the laws dictated that the correct information was the responsibility of the seller, and the penalty for not rectifying the situation could be quite harsh. Concerned when he could not locate the new owner to correct the registration document, Bob came to my office and asked that we pray that God would help him find the owner of the vehicle. I must confess that as I prayed with him, I did not share his childlike faith. Yet Bob walked out of my office completely confident that God would be his provider.

On his way back to work, Bob got caught in a major traffic jam that resulted in total gridlock. Waiting for the bottleneck to let up, he got out of his car to chat with the driver next to him. It was then that Bob recognized the wheels on the vehicle. It was his old car, which had been repainted! What were the odds that he would be stuck in traffic right next to his old vehicle—especially after having just asked God to help him find it? This was a concrete answer to prayer that the average skeptic would say was a mere coincidence. For Bob, however, this was God's miraculous provision—and it strengthened his faith all the more.

I eventually moved back to the United States and began conducting my meetings with Bob via telephone and e-mail conversations. After I had served as his long-distance spiritual guide and counselor for a year, Bob called to let me know that he wanted to purchase round-trip tickets to Latin America for my wife and me, so we could participate in the baptism of his entire family. As it turned out, we were scheduled to be in the city for other duties, so Bob scheduled a special baptismal service around my meetings. What a thrill and privilege it was to participate in that event—it was a modern-day scene straight out of the book of Acts.

Bob is now active in the service of the King and he regularly introduces his personal and professional acquaintances to Jesus Christ. He has taken the baton passed to him and is investing in the lives of seekers and fledgling Christians.

What I Learned from Bob

The key lesson God taught me through my relationship with Bob was that he divinely ordains the placement of people in our lives. We just need to use mentor's eyes to see opportunities that he has placed in our path and to have the purity of heart and the humility to be used as his instruments.

God placed John Mark and Saul into Barnabas's life and he had the mentor's eyes to see the potential for investing in these men. In addition, Barnabas exhibited the purity of heart and the humility to mentor John Mark and Saul. He didn't have any hidden or selfish agenda and he allowed his protégé (Paul) eventually to exceed him.

In my relationship with Bob, it was humbling to see God work in spite of my negative attitude at the start about my kids being traded. God had to open my mentor's eyes to see the opportunity before me—and then I had to humbly take on the mentor's mantle and allow God to work through me.

In the end, my own children (Millennials!) also benefited as they learned an incredible lesson by witnessing God's handiwork in the lives of Bob's family—all because they stuck to their commitment to stay on the baseball team (with a little nudging from Dad). They also experienced being God's instruments to accomplish his purpose.

Could You Be a Barnabas?

Do you yearn to make an impact on the Millennial generation the same way Barnabas left his mark on John Mark and Saul? Knowing all that you've learned through the pages of this book as well as in your own personal experience, do you believe that God is preparing you to have a unique mentoring ministry to tomorrow's adults?

I've attempted to teach and inspire you, my reader, through the power of stories; and it is in this same way that I've had my most effective connection with Millennials. Telling my personal stories to them was in essence opening my life to them (warts and all!). This took courage—I had to risk being vulnerable. However, I discovered it was *always* worth the risk because the results were inevitably more than what I could have hoped for.

Do you have a story to tell? Are you willing to risk being vulnerable by sharing some of your most poignant life experiences with the next generation? If you're willing to take the plunge, be ready to be used by God!

Ron Lee Davis, author of *Mentoring: The Strategy of the Master,* introduces the "mentor's maxim": *More time spent with fewer people equals greater lasting impact for God.*[4] The parable of the talents in Matthew 25 teaches the principle of investing the talents the Master gives us for his glory. Could it be that an investment in mentoring relationships, especially among Millennials, is the best way to invest our talents in light of eternity? I would respond with an emphatic yes.

At the beginning of this book, I relayed this Chinese proverb:

> If you are planting for a year, plant grain.
> If you are planting for a decade, plant trees.
> If you are planting for a century, plant people.[5]

My challenge to you in closing is to be about the business of planting people, investing your talents in an eternal legacy. What a privilege I've had in my own life to be used by God in this way. My prayer is that God will use you likewise to empower the next generation.

Notes

PREFACE

  1. Ron Lee Davis, *Mentoring: The Strategy of the Master* (Nashville: Thomas Nelson, 1991), p. 21.

CHAPTER ONE: LEAVING A LEGACY

  1. Brent Curtis and John Eldredge, *The Sacred Romance* (Nashville: Thomas Nelson, 1997), p. 23.

CHAPTER TWO: THE MILLENNIAL GENERATION

  1. Neil Howe and William Strauss, *Millennials Rising: The Next Great Generation* (New York: Random House, 2000), pp. 302-303.

  2. Howe and Strauss, pp. 302-303.

  3. Kim Painter, "The Sexual Revolution Hits Junior High," *USA Today*, 15-17 March 2002, pp. 1-2.

  4. Painter, pp. 1-2.

  5. Howe and Strauss, p. 4.

  6. Howe and Strauss, p. 7.

  7. Howe and Strauss, p. 35.

  8. Howe and Strauss, p. 77.

  9. Howe and Strauss, p. 51.

  10. Robert Putnam, "Bowling Alone: America's Declining Social Capital," *Journal of Democracy*, January 1995, p. 27.

  11. Howe and Strauss, p. 52.

12. Howe and Strauss, p. 52.

13. Bobb Biehl, *Mentoring: Confidence in Finding a Mentor and Becoming One* (Nashville: Broadman & Holman Publishers, 1996), p. 144.

14. Howe and Strauss, p. 347.

15. Barbara Kantrowitz and Keith Naughton, "Generation 9-11," *Newsweek,* 12 November 2001, p. 48.

16. Quoted by Kantrowitz and Naughton, p. 49.

17. Howe and Strauss, pp. 7-8.

18. Howe and Strauss, pp. 7-8.

19. Howe and Strauss, pp. 9-10.

20. Howe and Strauss, p. 164.

21. Howe and Strauss, p. 180.

22. Howe and Strauss, p. 180.

23. Wendy Murray Zoba, *Generation 2K: What Parents and Others Need to Know About the Millennials* (Downers Grove, Ill.: InterVarsity Press, 1999), p. 61.

24. Murray Zoba, p. 61.

25. "Teen-Sex Rate Drops for the First Time in 25 Years," *Religious News Service,* 1 May 1997, p. 3.

26. Barbara Risman and Pepper Schwartz, quoted by Karen S. Peterson, "Girls Stand Up to Boys," *USA Today,* 23 April 2002, 8D.

27. Howe and Strauss, p. 185.

28. Howe and Strauss, p. 185.

29. Howe and Strauss, p. 188.

30. Quoted by Wendy Murray Zoba, "Youth Has Special Powers," *Christianity Today,* 5 February 2001, p. 57.

31. Quoted by Murray Zoba, "Youth Has Special Powers," p. 57.

32. As cited by Murray Zoba, "Youth Has Special Powers," p. 57.

33. Murray Zoba, "Youth Has Special Powers," p. 57.

34. Murray Zoba, *Generation 2K*, p. 64.

35. Murray Zoba, *Generation 2K*, p. 65.

36. Liz Kelly, "Choir Girl," *CCM*, November 1998, p. 28.

37. Kristen Campbell, "Despite Some Negative Images, Teens Quietly Go about Doing Good," *Religious News Service*, 31 March 1997, p. 6.

38. Howe and Strauss, p. 216.

39. Howe and Strauss, p. 215.

40. President Franklin Roosevelt, speech accepting nomination for second term (June 27, 1936), as cited in Howe and Strauss, p. 352.

41. Kantrowitz and Naughton, p. 50.

42. Quoted by Kantrowitz and Naughton, p. 50.

43. Jerry Wunder, "Choosing a Different Legacy," Sunday message, March 10, 2002, Beijing International Christian Fellowship, Beijing, China.

CHAPTER THREE: THE LOST CHILDREN

1. "The Lost Children of Rockdale County," Rachel Dretzin Goodman and Barak Goodman, prod. and dir., *Frontline*, Public Broadcasting System, 19 October 1999, transcript p. 6.

2. "The Lost Children," p. 6.

3. "The Lost Children," p. 10.

4. "The Lost Children," p. 13.

5. "The Lost Children," p. 26.

6. "The Lost Children," p. 15.

7. "The Lost Children," p. 16.

8. "The Lost Children," p. 21.

9. "The Lost Children," p. 16.

10. "Producers' Interview: The Lessons of Conyers," Rachel Dretzin Goodman and Barak Goodman, prod. and dir., *Frontline,* Public Broadcasting System, 19 October 1999, transcript p. 1.

11. Paula Rinehart, "Losing Our Promiscuity," *Christianity Today,* 10 July 2000, p. 39.

12. Ron Powers, "The Apocalypse of Adolescence," *Atlantic Monthly,* March 2002, pp. 64-65.

13. Quoted by Powers, p. 65.

14. Powers, p. 74.

15. Josh McDowell, "Sounding the Alarm: The Urgent Message of PROJECT 911," *www.josh.org/project911/*josh.asp, accessed 21 March 2002.

16. McDowell.

17. Ronald P. Sykes, "School Climate: Building a Positive Learning Environment." Keynote presentation at the Conference for Chief School Administrators, Southern Association of Colleges and Schools, Altlanta, Ga., December 2, 1998.

18. Beth Ross, interviewed in "The Lost Children," transcript p. 7.

19. Dan Kindlon, interviewed by Bill O'Reilly, "The Corruption of the American Child," FOX Broadcasting Company, 28 March 2002.

20. Michael Josephson, interviewed by Bill O'Reilly.

21. Quoted by Wendy Murray Zoba, *Generation 2K: What Parents and Others Need to Know About the Millennials* (Downers Grove, Ill.: InterVarsity Press, 1999), pp. 73-74.

22. Claire Sterk, interviewed in "The Lost Children," transcript p. 12.

CHAPTER FOUR: THE FULL SPECTRUM

1. George Barna, *The Frog in the Kettle: What Christians Need to Know About Life in the Year 2000* (Ventura, Calif.: Regal, 1990), p. 123.

2. Todd Hahn, "The Post-modern Church," keynote address, IFMA/EFMA Personnel Conference, Colorado Springs, Colo., December 2, 1999.

3. Charles Colson, "Reaching the Pagan Mind," *Christianity Today,* 9 November 1992, p. 112.

4. Colson, p. 112.

5. George Barna, *The Barna Report: What Americans Believe* (Ventura, Calif.: Regal, 1991), pp. 83-85.

6. Barna, *The Barna Report*, pp. 83-85.

7. Gene Edward Veith Jr., *Postmodern Times: A Christian Guide to Contemporary Thought and Culture* (Wheaton, Ill.: Crossway Books, 1994), p. 18.

8. Veith, p. 20.

9. C. S. Lewis, *Mere Christianity* (New York: Macmillan, 1960), p. 19.

10. J. P. Moreland, *Love God with All Your Mind* (Colorado Springs, Colo.: NavPress, 1997), p. 43.

11. Charles Colson, "Post-Truth Society," *Christianity Today,* 11 March 2002, p. 112.

12. Colson, "Post-Truth Society," p. 112.

13. Veith, p. 229.

14. Stephen Benko, *Pagan Rome and the Early Christians* (Bloomington, Ind.: Indiana University Press, 1984), pp. 58-59.

15. Veith, p. 230.

16. Mona Charon, "What Did Lindh's Parents Expect?" *The Gazette* (Colorado Springs, Colo.), February 20, 2002, Metro 7.

17. Charon.

18. Charon.

19. Personal conversation with Todd Hahn, IFMA/EFMA Personnel Conference, Colorado Springs, Colo., December 2, 1999.

CHAPTER FIVE: UNDERSTANDING MENTORING

1. Ad placed by Hobby Lobby and Mardel Stores, *The Gazette* (Colorado Springs, Colo.), March 31, 2002, A7.

2. Leith Anderson, *A Church for the Twenty-First Century* (Minneapolis: Bethany House, 1992), pp. 45-46.

3. Gene Edward Veith Jr., *Postmodern Times: A Christian Guide to Contemporary Thought and Culture* (Wheaton, Ill.: Crossway Books, 1994), p. 227.

4. Josh McDowell, "Sounding the Alarm: the Urgent Message of PROJECT 911," *www.josh.org/project911/*josh.asp, accessed 21 March 2002.

5. Paul D. Stanley and J. Robert Clinton, *Connecting: The Mentoring Relationships You Need to Succeed in Life* (Colorado Springs, Colo.: NavPress, 1992), p. 40.

6. Stanley and Clinton, p. 43.

7. Donald A. Lichi, Ph.D., "Keeping Your Own Heart," 2002 ACSI International Administrator's Conference, Beatenburg, Switzerland, April 19, 2002.

8. Stanley and Clinton, p. 165.

9. The following descriptions of the three levels of mentoring and of each mentoring style are borrowed from Stanley and Clinton, p. 42.

10. Philip Yancey, *What's So Amazing About Grace?* (Grand Rapids, Mich.: Zondervan, 1997), p. 146.

CHAPTER SIX: PASSIVE MENTORING

1. Dr. Vernard Gant, lunch interview, Colorado Springs, Colo., April 8, 2002.

2. Paul D. Stanley and J. Robert Clinton, *Connecting: The Mentoring Relationships You Need to Succeed in Life* (Colorado Springs, Colo.: NavPress, 1992), p. 137.

3. Stanley and Clinton, p. 147.

4. Larry Crabb, *Shattered Dreams: God's Unexpected Pathway to Joy* (Colorado Springs, Colo.: WaterBrook Press, 2001), pp. 85-86.

5. Brent Curtis and John Eldredge, *The Sacred Romance* (Nashville: Thomas Nelson, 1997), p. 41.

6. Ideas from this paragraph were borrowed from Crabb, pp. 155-159.

CHAPTER NINE: MENTORING LESSONS

1. Laura Rabb and Bobby Clinton, *Barnabas, Encouraging Exhorter: A Study in Mentoring* (Altadena, Calif.: Barnabas Resources, 1985), p. 19.

2. Rabb and Clinton, p. 33.

3. Leighton Ford, *Transforming Leadership: Jesus' Way of Creating Vision, Shaping Values, and Empowering Change* (Downers Grove, Ill.: InterVarsity, 1991), p. 24.

4. Ron Lee Davis, *Mentoring: The Strategy of the Master* (Nashville: Thomas Nelson, 1991), p. 21.

5. Davis, p. 21.

About the Author

DR. DANIEL EGELER grew up on an isolated island in Lake Victoria, Tanzania, where his father was an "island evangelist." It was here that he learned the art of relating oral history from his African elders. Upon his return to the United States, he received a bachelor's degree from The King's College (NY), a master's degree from Washington State University (WA), and a doctorate in administration and instructional leadership from the University of Alabama (AL). Dan currently serves as the director for international school services (Europe and Africa) for the Association of Christian Schools International in Colorado Springs, Colorado. Dr. Egeler and his wife, Kathy, have four children: Andrew, Danielle, Matthew, and Bethany. They live in Colorado Springs.

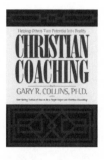
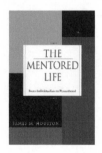